TIME OF HEALING

DAVID B. SMITH

Pacific Press® Publishing Association
Nampa, Idaho
Oshawa, Ontario, Canada
www.pacificpress.com

Edited by Jerry D. Thomas
Cover Design and Art by Justinen Creative Group
Inside Design by Steve Lanto

Additional copies of this book may be purchased at
http://www.adventistbookcenter.com

ISBN: 0-8163-1912-X

02 03 04 05 • 5 4 3 2 1

Contents

Jar of Tears 4

CHAPTER 1 Terror in the Skies 5

CHAPTER 2 The Savior Who Weeps 14

CHAPTER 3 Don't Be "Meek," Mr. President! 26

CHAPTER 4 How Mad Is God Right About Now? 39

CHAPTER 5 We Don't Lose Wars! 50

CHAPTER 6 Where Were You Tuesday Morning, God? 60

CHAPTER 7 Needing a Hiding Place 76

CHAPTER 8 Why Does God Let It Hurt? .86

CHAPTER 9 I Like It in This Fiery Furnace! 99

CHAPTER 10 Temporary Triumphs Against Terrorism 111

CHAPTER 11 "Thank God Life Is Unfair!" 124

Jar of Tears

My father told me once about a jar—
A jar God keeps to hold our tears.
It's in a special place up there in heaven;
He uses it to catch our pain and tears.

But, Dad, today that jar's not big enough
To hold the tears of this new world.
God weeps with us—it overflows.
Lives are changed—stained flags unfurled.

A nation prays for all its heroes
For mothers, fathers, sisters, brothers
For rescue workers, sons and daughters
For loss of friends and all the others.

What can we do? How can we help?
One voice lifts to the sky.
Together we will make it through;
Peace will triumph and replace our cry.
We can sing a song or say a prayer
Or tell someone about God's jar of tears.
We can hold a hand or say we care.
Let's reach out to touch and calm the fears.

O America, land of the brave,
Freedom's ring will long be heard.
No evil threat—no man or group
Will take our spirit, heart or word.

America, America,
God shed His grace on thee,
And crown thy good with brotherhood
From sea to shining sea.

My father told me once about a jar—
A jar God keeps to hold our tears . . .

Connie Vandeman Jeffery—9/15/01

1

Terror in the Skies

It's the same thing they said about Pearl Harbor. And November 22, 1963. You remember where you were when it happened.

I had just stumbled out of bed that Tuesday morning, September 11, and was getting ready to go for my early morning run when I happened to turn on CNN. At first my unfocused eyes made me think I was watching something from the History Channel or perhaps news from some foreign capital. Then the realizations began to hit like deadly dominos: the World Trade Center towers, the Pentagon, the grassy field in Pennsylvania, the imploding skyscrapers, the specter of thousands of deaths.

The question even Billy Graham cannot answer in the stark, stone silence of the National Cathedral in Washington, D. C., is this: *Where was God when this happened?* Did the heavenly Father of these victims take a break on September 11, 2001? There are supposed to be, in all the world's airports, security measures. X-ray machines. Sky marshals. Doors that can be opened only by authorized personnel. Planes that can be boarded only by the Good People. And then there's supposed to be a loving Deity named God. Where in the universe was this Person who promises to protect His children?

It took a few days, but we soon learned that nine members in my own Seventh-day Adventist faith community had perished in the conflagration. Many courageous firefighters were following the commands of the Scripture to rescue others—and lost their lives doing so. People up on the ninetieth floor were going about their activities, remembering the verses they had read earlier on the subway, the prayers they had prayed. They had confessed God as their Protector, and that Protector now stood by while they died. Why?

Intelligence agencies confessed during the dark days to follow, that this evil fantasy—flying commercial wide-body jets, fully loaded with jet fuel, into America's tallest skyscrapers—simply had never occurred to them. Donald Rumsfeld, the Secretary of Defense, admitted to *Meet the Press*'s Tim Russert, that no one had dreamed of something so evil.

But there was One who knew all along, and that was God. And He's *supposed* to know! So the question burns within us. Where was God at 8:48 A.M.? Why weren't prayers of Christians answered on that bleak day? When good kids like Rodney Dickens, an eleven-year-old boy who won a field trip to the Channel Islands National Marine Sanctuary in California, pray with their parents for protection for the day, for angels to be with them and guard their footsteps . . . what happened? He and his two fellow winners, along with three outstanding teachers sponsored by the National Geographic Society, all boarded one of the doomed flights and perished in a fiery ball.

Does the angel promise of Psalm 34:7 mean anything or doesn't it? When cell phones and beepers worked so immediately, so efficiently, on that dark Tuesday, as survivors out on the sidewalks outside the World Trade Center successfully dialed to tell spouses they were safe, why didn't prayers get through? That old song "Operator, get me Jesus on the line" seems rather hollow now as families of Christian victims attend the funerals and wonder why phone lines work and prayer lines don't.

That's the hardest question in the world to answer, and it's inappropriate for those of us who watched from the safe sidelines to give glib answers. But it's a fact of this planet's sin-soaked history that murderers have very often been allowed to murder. Clear back in the fourth chapter of the Bible, when there were only four people walking around on this earth, one of them picked up a weapon and bludgeoned another one to death. And there were only four people for God to keep track of! Not the tens of thousands who were moving their way through the World Trade Center towers. Not six billion, which is what heaven is supposed to be protecting now. Just four! And yet the all-powerful Lord of all creation stood by, silent, unmoving, His power masked, His defensive prowess hidden away, while a resentful terrorist named Cain killed his fellow human being in the first attack ever recorded.

Somehow, even in the darkness of not understanding, not knowing why, the human race still seeks God. On that terrible, dark Tuesday, millions of people moved wordlessly to the churches. Not just to memorialize the lost and to pay tribute to the heroes, many at that time still unknown to an anxious world. But also to seek this hidden God. To assure themselves that He was still there, watching from the shadows of the Empire State Building and the Statue of Liberty. We all know in our hearts that somehow, for reasons we don't yet understand, God permits the things that cause Him a greater ache than anyone else feels. Preachers everywhere, not just in the Big Apple, struggled to find words to express what we all know inside: God is still good. God is still love. God weeps too.

"Why did this happen?" the media wanted to know. "Where was God?"

"You could see Him in the selfless people who patiently helped injured coworkers down eighty flights of stairs, even as the World Trade Center towers were ablaze and moments from collapsing," writes Mark Finley. "You could see Him in the scores of firefighters and police officers who unhesitatingly rushed into harm's way at the scene and then were buried when the buildings collapsed. You could see God in all the people who rushed to give blood or make donations or volunteer their time."

Even with our hearts filled with such hurt, we're invited to look soberly at the big picture. God had—and still has—an Eden plan for this world. A plan with no death, no sin, no explosions, no swastikas, no "cell groups," no guns, no bullets, no funerals. But for now, for a very long time now, our world has been held by an enemy named Lucifer. And it's clear in Genesis, then again in Job, and yet again in Revelation (which describes the generation of 2001 and beyond), that God does permit the blueprint of the dragon named Satan to be manifested here. There's such a thing as free choice, liberty of conscience, the power to choose. People are invited to ally themselves with God, but they're also permitted to swear allegiance to Satan. Babies are born pure and innocent, but as they grow up and reach the age of accountability, God doesn't force them into a straitjacket of holiness, of unthinking good behavior. Young men grow up into their teen years and choose to enter the service of an Osama bin Laden. God allows them to sign up with a terrorist organization. And then to pick up box cutters, take over a 767 airplane, and use it as an enormous flying bomb.

God, our heavenly Father, plans for good . . . but permits evil. Sin and death were never part of His creation blueprint for Earth, but He allowed one of His created beings, an angel named Lucifer, to lie and deceive and rebel and even kill. The Creator God very clearly communicated with heaven's residents and with Adam and Eve and with their descendants, that sin and death were inseparable curses. One would lead to the other. And then He permitted them both for a certain length of time that only He knows.

In the aftermath of September 11, we cannot fully understand the end from the beginning and grasp why God permits this lengthy demonstration. Why did God permit Mohamed Atta and Marwan al-Shehhi to choose the terrorism route? That's free will. Which, until the end of the experiment called sin, is permitted to continue here.

The human race cannot reply satisfactorily to all questions, but we can know one thing with absolute assurance: God fixes it all in the end. The rubble from New York City and random school shootings are not only eliminated, but fixed. God completely repairs what went so tragically wrong in America on September 11, 2001. Not by clearing away the piles of debris and rebuilding those magnificent edifices, but by restoring *lives*. Those victims can live again. Tom Burnett can rejoin his wife Deena; Jeremy Glick and his wife, Lyzbeth can stand as a couple again. Lisa Beamer stood in the House chambers as President Bush paid tribute to her husband, Todd Beamer, who, together with Tom and Jeremy and unknown others, resisted the terrorists aboard United Airlines Flight 93 and saved countless lives. God can reunite that family and then eternally protect them.

So many people right now must have it just tear at them—*Can't we simply go back in time? I won't let my beloved go to work; we'll stay home from that Boston-L.A. trip we'd planned. I'll have my wife call in sick; the Pentagon can do without her.* To simply erase September 11 from all world calendars. To have back the innocence, the carefree simple joys of pre-terrorist life. To have those friends back again, with their smiles, the banter, having a cup of coffee together in the World Trade Center towers. Relatives and friends would sacrifice anything they possibly could to spin back the clock and have their loved ones safely in their arms again. But death seems so permanent, so forever, so unfixable.

Maybe you recall a New Testament story in which Jesus arrives at the site of a funeral. Already four days have gone by since the death of His good friend Lazarus. And Lazarus's sisters, Mary and Martha, are wild with grief. Where had Jesus been?

Why hadn't He hurried? Even Jesus can't turn the clock back and give them their brother back. Even Jesus can't create a time tunnel and turn death into life. But Christ calmly walks with them to the tomb, says a prayer, calls Lazarus back to life, and then smiles. "Unwrap him and let him go," Jesus says. Problem solved. Death destroyed. For Jesus it's so easy.

And what Jesus did for Lazarus and for his grieving family that day is *real*. This is a true story. It's not a fable, a fairy tale, or one of the great legends. A man was dead for four days . . . and Jesus, with absolute assurance, brought him back to life. And what Jesus did in Bethany 2,000 years ago, He is equally capable of doing now in New York City and Arlington National cemeteries. The Bible promises in His own words: "I am the resurrection, and the life: he that believeth in me, though he were dead, yet shall he live" (John 11:25).

That promise of our Savior and Friend, Jesus, is absolutely true. And here's an additional word of comfort. What happened on that Tuesday—Jesus knows all about it.

There's not a friend like the lowly Jesus,
 No, not one! No, not one! . . .
Jesus *knows* all about our struggles,
He will guide till the day is done.

In the Lazarus story, Jesus told the disciples that Lazarus's illness was "not unto death" and waited two days before beginning the journey to Judea. While they were still on the road, Jesus told the disciples that Lazarus was dead. He used the word *sleeping*, but "dead" is what He meant. How did Christ know His friend was gone? How did He know? There were no news reports, no cell phones or faxes. The earlier messenger had simply said: "Lazarus is sick." How did Jesus have this latest update? Because He just *knows*. Whatever grief you're feeling today, Jesus already knows. There's no friend like the lowly—and loving and all-knowing—Jesus.

Sometimes at a funeral, or following a tragic holocaust, some are tempted to decide on their own, or even publicly announce, who among the dead were "saved." Only Jesus knows. Jesus the merciful Savior and God the loving Judge know everything. And we don't.

Maybe you've been to a funeral for a friend who died in the September 11 attacks, and you have no knowledge that this person had ever said a specific and definite "Yes" to the claims of Jesus Christ. Had the gospel message ever been placed directly in his or her path? Had he ever experienced a firm yes-or-no encounter with the claims of God or literally heard Joshua's invitation: "Choose you this day whom ye will serve" (Joshua 24:15)? As far as you know, he never did . . . and so your heart is gripped with the fear that his salvation went up in the flames of New York.

Let me encourage you today to leave all such concerns in the loving care of Jesus—even when it comes to the hijackers, whose faces we saw in grainy black-and-white security-camera photos. Some Islamic fundamentalists promised that the hijackers would immediately enter Paradise, while other responsible theologians countered that the pure teachings of Islam condemn the killing of innocent people and plainly state that those who commit such murders will not even *smell* Paradise.

But God knows all things. We don't. What kind of confusion, loneliness, despair, or early life experiences would have led to such grievous and wicked decisions as these men made? God knows all the factors. We don't. And God's love and wisdom are so much greater than ours, that when it comes to judgment, our best response is simply prayer. Probably *silent* prayer. Silent, united prayers to tell God that we trust in Him to fix this incomprehensible wrong.

And that determination is rapidly sweeping the globe today. Millions who gather to pray are holding fast to their faith—for many, a newfound faith—that God is the only solution, the only Father with power to completely fix broken things. September 11 and today and always, He's our strength and our only hope.

The question to ask ourselves is this: Why do we take so long to learn this lesson? Why does the human race seem to lurch blindly from one crisis to the next one, packing the churches for a few days or weeks, and then lapsing back into the comfortable life of before, as soon as the airports once again permit curbside check-in?

You would think that most of the world would at last look up at heaven and say to God: "All right! We GET IT! We see that sin is evil and righteousness is good. We understand now that Lucifer's plan is deadly, and Yours is life eternal, life abundant. At last we comprehend that the wages of sin are death, that violence breeds violence, that for humankind to go its own way is a slow suicide. God, at long last, why don't You COME? And rescue us all! Because after these past 6,000 years, at last WE GET IT!"

I know that many times I've prayed in earnestness and almost frustration because it all seemed so clear. This is the unspoken anguish behind the Christian's "Maranatha" prayer. God, we GET it! We're slow and spiritually stupid, but not *that* stupid. After the Holocaust and then Rwanda and then Kosovo and babies born with AIDS and now this—Pearl Harbor II—it's painfully clear, agonizingly clear, that Satan's agenda for this world is nothing but mass suicide.

And as the world watched this unfolding drama "America At War," there have been signs that we might be slowly learning. Churches are filling up. People stand together in their grief. They reach out for some shred of faith, some assurance that death is not the end, that these funerals are not the final chapter. Filmmakers are rethinking what they produce; network television executives are saying to each other: "Shouldn't we cancel that violent, cynical series that seemed such a red-hot ratings winner before September 11?"

And yet, here's the reality we have to try to understand: Tragedy hit . . . and so everyone went to church. With buildings imploding and approximately 5,000 people simply vaporizing, and with a trillion dollars vanishing out of the Dow Jones near-collapse, this planet reached out to God on September 11, 2001.

But what about on September 10? On September 8 I was in church, preaching from God's Word that Saturday morning, and it was to a small gathering. Many were at the beach or in their backyards or still in bed. Was it clear to everyone the weekend *before* the hijackings that to live in relationship with God is the best way, the only way? Or do we understand the goodness of God only when the evilness of the world is thrust into our living rooms on CNN? Does the devil have to shoot right at us before we turn our eyes to heaven? And really, perhaps this is what God is waiting for. Even after Auschwitz and Bosnia and Littleton, Colorado, so few people still seek an abiding relationship with God *all the time,* not just during a crisis.

For years preachers have both joked and lamented about what they call "C & E Christians." People who show up at church just for Christmas and Easter. They don't want a daily relationship with God; they just want to say hello—and goodbye—during the two major church holidays. And now maybe we have "T & S Christianity," which gets people to church only following terrorist attacks and shootings. We enter the house of our invisible heavenly Father only when our hearts are aching from a firefighter's funeral. But when the hurts fade, we return to our previous routines.

In his book with the challenging title *Disappointment With God,* Philip Yancey writes about how the children of Israel had what we so often seem to demand. God showed Himself to them! He was real! He was right there! He gave them signs and wonders. They heard His voice booming from the mountaintop. They saw His manna every morning; they drank miracle water which He provided from the rock. And yet, they really looked His direction only when they were hungry. Or when the water ran out. Or when the locusts or the Philistines swooped down on them. So few of them seemed to want God *all the time* (pp. 42, 43). Unless there was a shooting or a tragedy or a falling skyscraper, they went their own way. The relationship was unendingly shallow, marked just by the little moments of crisis connection.

So there could be a silver lining from the Manhattan tragedy. As people seek God now, during a crisis, will they stay with Him as the crisis passes? Healing will be slow in the Big Apple, but it will come. What then? Will the prayers slowly disperse as the memories fade? Will church attendance revert to normal? Or, as we dry our tears and begin going to Disney World again, will we learn that to seek God *all* the time is the only way to lasting wholeness?

In the book of Revelation, we find page after page of blood-soaked sorrow. Earthquakes and famines and death—the seven last plagues and a great tribulation. The scarred landscape of New York City is just a foreshadowing of what might be yet to come. People living then will have a mass crisis of faith: seeking God and not finding Him. But through it all there is a group of people who don't seek God just when things are bad. Plagues are raining down, but that's not the motivation for their devotion. No, it says in Revelation 14:4: They "follow the Lamb wherever He goes" (NKJV).

Pastor Morris Venden has a sermon in which he asks the congregation, in their imaginations, to attend that Judgment Day gathering when the "sheep and the goats" face their moment of destiny. And someone outside the kingdom stands up in protest. "God, You let me get cancer! Nobody ever offered me a break! I wanted to get well, but no, I didn't get any help. This is unfair!"

But very quietly, without fanfare, a person inside the New Jerusalem steps forward and tells a similar story. He had cancer too. The battle was fierce for him as well. And despite his prayers, God allowed him to face this unseen foe right to the end. He, too, died after a long battle. And the rebel's charge that God is unfair dies away.

Others might protest from outside the New Jerusalem that his kids were killed in tragic car accidents. Or in a schoolyard shooting. Or that her husband needlessly died while faithfully doing his job at the Pentagon. Where was God? Why didn't He rescue them? Was heaven picking on them just because they weren't born-again Christians who went to church fifty-two times a year? The accusations stand thick in the air.

But again, one of God's loyal followers stands up. Maybe it's the Tomlin family. They went with their son John to Mexico for a mission trip in 1998; they worked side by side with him to build a house for poor people there. Certainly on Tuesday morning, April 20, 1999, that God-fearing family knelt around the kitchen table and committed their lives to Jesus. They placed their destinies in God's hands, as I'm sure they still do every single day of the year. Just a few hours later, this handsome sixteen-year-old Christian was a fallen corpse in the hallways of Columbine High School. Rachel Scott was dead. Born-again Christian Cassie Bernall, who had been rescued from an occult lifestyle just two years earlier, was dead. And the parents of these precious kids stand up to tell their stories. Their loved ones died too.

Does that mean God never answered their prayers? Did He ignore them? Did He turn a deaf ear to their petitions on Tuesday, April 20? Was God on a distant holiday on the morning of September 11, 2001? So many surviving family members will stand up and testify with great courage that they continue to trust in God. That they believe in God, even when they can't understand His purposes. They'll testify that when the great throngs crowded into the churches for these funerals, that God was there too. God mourned too.

As students wrote farewell messages on Rachel Scott's white casket after the Littleton massacre, I'm sure God's invisible hand shook with emotion as He wrote His own agonizing words of love. Rachel's mother wrote: "Honey, you are everything a mother could ever ask the Lord for in a daughter. I love you so much! Mom." Did God not read those words? Did He not care? God's cries are the most wrenching of all. The Bible tells us that in the end God will wipe away all tears . . . including His own. Believe me, He will have to begin with His own.

This brings us back to today. How should *we* pray? Jesus prayed, "Thy will be done" and knew that His heavenly Father loved Him enough to always give the answer that, in the eternal scheme of things, would be the right one and the best one.

So friend, let's pray. As these brave champions of faith who bury the dead in New York and Washington pray . . . let us all pray together.

2

The Savior Who Weeps

Maybe you remember a classic episode of *The Mary Tyler Moore Show*, where veteran actress Betty White played the obnoxious, pompous, insensitive Sue Ann Nivens. This Nivens character was despised by the rest of the team at WJM Television, and finally one of them got up their courage and cut her down to size, gave her a real tongue-lashing.

The scene happened during a black-tie dinner where Betty White's character was supposed to receive some media award for her Happy Homemaker show. But now she was in tears. "How can I go up there on the platform like this?" she wailed. "I'm a mess; I'm a wreck." There was no way she could go on. Of course, with TV's impeccable timing, the emcee chose that exact moment to announce: "And the winner: Sue Ann Nivens."

And this forlorn, weeping woman slowly makes her way among the tables to the front of the ballroom, with Mary and Lou Grant and Murray and Ted all watching anxiously from the sidelines. What have they done? How can she cry and deliver her Thank-you speech simultaneously? And the kicker happens when she gets to the microphone. Because all at once—*voilà!*—a thousand rays of sunshine light her up. "I'd like to thank my millions of fans, and all of Minneapolis, and my beloved friends at WJM."

And it's as though the tears had never happened. She could turn them on, and she could turn them off.

Are the tears of God real? When those planes plummeted from the sky and struck the twin towers at 300 knots, and Jesus cried, were His tears genuine? Or *did* He cry that day along with us?

One of the most unforgettable sermons I ever heard came from the lips of the incomparable veteran preacher Charles Bradford. It was at a General Conference session in my Adventist denomination, and he is a true keynoter of keynoters. This was back a few years, when Lee Majors and Lindsay Wagner had brought the word *bionic* into our American vocabulary. And Bradford, speaking so eloquently about the heart of Jesus, the sympathy of our Savior, rose to a crescendo with this observation: "I'm glad my Jesus wasn't a bionic man," he said, "a man with eyes of glass. No, Jesus had eyes that could weep!"

And really, that is tremendous news. The Bible shares several accounts where Jesus cried, shed tears. But why did He? Were they real tears?

The story believers think of immediately is related in the Gospel of John, chapter 11. Trivia lovers know that the shortest verse in all of Scripture is, "Jesus wept."

It's appropriate to call into question the genuineness of these tears, because it was common in that Oriental culture for relatives to actually hire professional mourners. The family would have paid experts, a whole gallery section of Sue Ann Nivens–types who could turn on the tears and give you a Niagara Falls of pseudo-grief.

If you study the original Greek language, verse 33 talks about Mary and these hired mourners weeping, and the word *klaio* is used, indicating this kind of demonstrative wailing—which might be genuine, or it might be for five shekels an hour. However, in verse 35, where Jesus Himself weeps, we find in contrast the word *dakruo*. And that very clearly means "to shed tears." So Jesus wasn't a gifted politician who just scrunched up His face for a television camera. Here in this pain-filled story, Jesus was actually crying; He was crying for real.

And yet we have to ask another question. Jesus is at a funeral and He cries. Well and good. But in Bethany, Christ is just a few minutes away, and only nine verses away in this story, from one of the great resurrection sagas of all time. Probably the second most dramatic ever, after His own. And He knows that. He knows He's going to bring His friend back to life. In fact, the very casualness of His rescue trip to Bethany, almost dawdling, hanging around where He was for two whole days after getting the telegram before starting out, shows that He's being very intentional about allowing the scene to play out this way. So are these tears at the funeral just a show?

It says in verse 33: "When Jesus saw [Mary] weeping, and the Jews who had come along with her also weeping, he was deeply moved in spirit and troubled" (NIV).

Have you had that experience at a funeral, where perhaps you didn't really know the deceased? I didn't know a single person who died in the terrorist attacks—and yet I burst into tears many, many times as I watched television. And what a beautiful thing to see it happen here! Jesus saw the tears of His precious friend Mary. He knew that her heart was breaking. He was able to distinguish the false tears from the real ones and to commiserate with her. And all at once He finds Himself crying too. With the resurrection just minutes away, with a party about to begin, Jesus still weeps at this moment.

The book *The Desire of Ages,* by nineteenth-century author Ellen G. White, paints a meaningful word picture of the tears of Jesus: "Though He was the Son of God, yet He had taken human nature upon Him, and He was moved by human sorrow. His tender, pitying heart is ever awakened to sympathy by suffering. He weeps with those that weep, and rejoices with those that rejoice" (page 533).

You've probably heard that old song "You'll Never Walk Alone." We find here that we will never *weep* alone either. When we cry at funerals, Jesus cries too. Our loss of loved ones on those hijacked jets is keenly felt by Heaven as well.

But there's a second emotion hiding in here, a deeper level to the tears of Jesus. The King James Version says in verse 33 that Christ "groaned in the spirit," that He was troubled. But *The Message* paraphrase by Eugene Peterson describes the scene like this: "When Jesus saw her sobbing and the Jews with her sobbing, a deep *anger* welled up within him" (emphasis supplied).

Why is Jesus angry? He spotted the hypocrisy in the crowd, the fake tears of some. After all, some of these same people who were weeping and wailing would be plotting His own crucifixion, that would take place in just a few days.

But Jesus was angry for a bigger reason. He didn't hate those phony mourners; they were just doing their job. Perhaps the funeral for His friend, that one graveside moment, was to Jesus a summing-up, a piling-up of all the funerals, all the needless, senseless Omaha Beach deaths, the accumulation of Osama bin Laden monstrosities throughout the history of the world. "Lord, if You had been here, my brother would not have died." And maybe Jesus, with tears streaming down His own face, wanted to say in return: "Listen, if this planet hadn't lurched off course and gone down the wrong path of sin, *nobody* would have ever died! *Nobody!* Every single funeral on this planet is the most wretched, needless, wasted, unnecessary, tragic, useless experience there is! In My Father's kingdom, there is none of this!"

In that same book, *The Desire of Ages,* Ellen White takes that same view: "It was not only because of the scene before Him that Christ wept. The weight of the grief of ages was upon Him." Then she adds this second insight: "He saw the terrible effects of the transgression of God's law. He saw that in the history of the world, beginning with the death of Abel, the conflict between good and evil had been unceasing. Looking down the years to come, He saw the suffering and sorrow, tears and death, that were to be the lot of men. His heart was pierced with the pain of the human family of all ages and in all lands. The woes of the sinful race were heavy upon His soul, and the fountain of His tears was broken up as He longed to relieve all their distress" (page 534).

What's the last funeral you were at? I believe Jesus, there in Bethany, sensed *that* funeral too. He tuned in from A.D. 31 as Dan Rather, Tom Brokaw, and Peter Jennings explained the horrific footage from our nation's capital and from New York City's ruptured skyline, and it made Him righteously angry. He shed tears, friend, for you too. He cried for all of it that day—and for all of us.

Real tears. Real anger. Real love. Because Jesus is a Real Friend.

A few years ago Thomas Youk, just fifty-two years old, died on camera, as the CBS news magazine *60 Minutes,* hosted by Mike Wallace, recorded his last moments for a nationwide viewing audience. The death was the work of Dr. Jack Kevorkian, called by some an angel of mercy and described by others as Dr. Death.

More than a hundred people have now died with his help, either by carbon monoxide gas or by intravenous poisoning, using his traveling machine, the

"Mercitron." A *Reader's Digest* article by John Corry describes the now incarcerated Kevorkian as being eager to establish himself as the "Domino's of death," able to deliver his service "like a pizza" (April 1999, p. 90).

Does this man have true compassion for the elderly, for the terminally ill? What does this word *compassion* actually mean? In Latin, we have *com* and *pati*, meaning "to suffer *with*." And in biblical Greek, the word *sympathy* derives from *syn* and *pathos*, also meaning "to feel or suffer *with*." Does Kevorkian suffer with his clients? Or has he always just been fascinated with death itself, as evidenced by his long history of wanting to experiment on consenting death-row inmates, of his stalking hospital corridors, looking for patients who were near the end of their lives? Is that the extent of his caring?

In *The Jesus I Never Knew*, Philip Yancey discusses the ability of God to reach down and relate to us. He tells two agonizing stories of betrayal and hurt: one involving a blind man whose wife had an affair with a friend right in their own home. In the second, a youth pastor lost his wife and baby daughter to AIDS. So where was God? Did God understand? "Does God care?" Yancey writes. "I know of only one way to answer that question, and it has come through my study of the life of Jesus. In Jesus, God gave us a face, and I can read directly in that face how God feels about people like the youth pastor and the blind man who never gave me his name. By no means did Jesus eliminate all suffering—He healed only a few in one small patch of the globe—but He did signify an answer to the question of whether God cares" (p. 159).

The book of Mark reveals yet another picture of Jesus' sympathy for people. In chapter 6 Christ and His disciples simply had to get away for some quiet time, for some desperately needed R & R. "Let's go find an isolated spot in the wilderness," He said to His followers, "where we can be alone to talk and get some rest."

However, just three verses later, the people, the crowds, were so eager for help and for healing and for teaching that they hiked along the lake to find Him. And in verse 34 is a beautiful picture of our sympathetic Friend: "When Jesus landed and saw a large crowd, he had compassion on them, because they were like sheep without a shepherd. So he began teaching them many things" (NIV).

Back in 1957, when I was just a two-year-old, my dad was entertaining a call to be a missionary way up in northern Thailand, 500 miles north of

Bangkok. As he and Mom—with their three very small boys—were considering whether or not they should go, a plaintive letter came from the Christian volunteer who was trying to hold the mission work together in the town of Chiang Mai. And the letter basically said this: "Please come. Pastor Smith, please do come." And then this heart-stopping line: "Out here we are like sheep without a shepherd."

The letter was probably in broken English, but the Thai word for *sheep* is something like this: *Gha*. And this earnest letter said to the young American minister: "We are just *gha*—we're lost, lonely lambs. The gospel is so new to us; we need someone to lead us." And Dad, who lived in the comfort of California with a pretty wife and a college diploma on the walls of his study, got on a merchant ship—the *Steel Admiral*—and took the dirty, exhausting, six-week journey to Thailand . . . because he had compassion and wanted to be a shepherd to these lambs.

That's the tiniest picture, a human replication, of what Jesus Christ feels for us every single day. For our lostness, Jesus has compassion. He feels *for* us and *with* us. In the same story of Jesus having compassion on the multitude, He also notices their physical needs: "These people are hungry. They haven't eaten all day. We've got to feed them." His sympathy even extended to their growling stomachs, their need for a bit of supper. And He miraculously provided 5,000 instant meals.

No matter who I am or where I am or what I've been through, I have a Friend named Jesus who understands. That's not just a sermon; it's not a rhyme. It's not a poem. In the days when slavery was still practiced in the United States, the slaves would sing a song that began, "Nobody knows the trouble I've seen. Nobody knows but Jesus."

Was that just a good song? Or was it the gritty, tangible truth? Had Jesus ever felt the sting of the lash? Yes, He did. You can read about it in John 19:1. Did Jesus ever get called names, have people make fun of Him? Go back to verse 29. He was born without a legitimate human father—and somebody pointed that out to Him every single day of His life.

Do you ever feel unappreciated? Just imagine what Jesus went through in that arena!

In that same book, *The Jesus I Never Knew,* Yancey reminds us how we sometimes cry out at an unforgiving universe: "I didn't choose to be born!" Which is true. And then he adds this observation: "Alone of all people in history, [Jesus] had the privilege of *choosing* where and when to be born" (p. 50).

And we say: "Lucky Him! I didn't get to pick and choose; fate thrust me into this mess, but Jesus got to pick His place and time." Ah, but notice how Jesus willfully placed Himself right into the very spot in history where He would be subjected to all the pain we feel. Born into poverty, into dirt, into a manger. Born into humanness and temptation. Born into a pagan empire, into a world where stonings and crucifixions and terrorist attacks were the common fixes for what He was going to offer. Does Jesus understand? He purposefully put Himself where He would have no choice *but* to understand.

Speaking of Dr. Jack Kevorkian, Yancey thinks about the ways that Jesus understands our hurts, the ways that He cries with us and sheds tears of true compassion, and then closes with this: "As a doctor who works in hospice told me, 'When my patients pray, they are talking to someone who has actually died—something that's not true of any other adviser, counselor, or death expert' " (p. 271)

Kevorkian for years has put on his business cards "Jack Kevorkian, M.D. Bioethics and Obitiatry. Special death counseling. By appointment only." He's a self-proclaimed expert in "obitiatry," the doctoring of death. He's an expert in death; he's done a lot of research, much of it morbid. But how expert is he really? Has he ever *died?* Has he experienced death? What's more to the point, has he conquered it like Jesus has? Jesus went to the cross, which was no Mercitron potassium-chloride joy ride. And He came through in victory on the other side.

But this forces us to address a vital biblical doctrine with great caution and humility. How does God feel today, right now, about our Christian funerals? When we say goodbye at the cemetery and are weeping, filled with grief, does God join us in that grief, just as Jesus did at the funeral of Lazarus?

Maybe you've read the wrenching story going back to November 22, 1963. Here in America, almost every citizen of the nation knew, 99.8% of us, along with most of the world, that President John F. Kennedy had been killed by a sniper's bullet. Within minutes, we all knew. Except for two small children who didn't know. Caroline and John, Jr.—John-John—had not been told. Jackie, their mother, was on her way back to Washington,

D.C. on Air Force One with the body of the President in a coffin. She couldn't do it. And finally it fell to the children's White House nurse, Miss Shaw, to break the news to the kids. One at a time. And very carefully, with her heart breaking, the nanny took six-year-old Caroline on her lap and explained that a bad man had shot her daddy. The doctors had tried to make him better, but had failed. And then she put it like this: "Your daddy went up to heaven to be with Patrick." The Kennedys, you remember, had lost a son at childbirth the previous August. "Patrick needed your daddy so bad, and now he's with him."

A book entitled *Letters From Heaven* has a message from above which begins like this: "Dear child of God, Today we welcomed your father into heaven! I wish you could have seen his look of wonder and joy. Still, I know how deeply grieved you and your mother are at this time."

These anecdotes seem to tell us that while our hearts are heavy with grief here on earth, Heaven is in the opposite mode—one of celebration. What is parting for us is reunion for Heaven. We cry and God laughs. We are shedding tears, but Jesus, up in heaven, is not shedding tears because the soul of the one we miss is immediately up there with Him.

Now friend, I have to proceed in these next few lines with such respect for the beliefs each of us brings to this issue. I honor your Bible convictions; I praise God for what you may have studied or how you might have been taught. But allow me to suggest—just prayerfully suggest—that the Bible's teachings don't paint a picture of *grief here* and *joy there*. Or that our separation is Heaven's reunion.

Stay right here in this Lazarus story: John 11. Jesus doesn't say to His disciples: "Lazarus has died and gone to heaven." No, He simply remarks: " 'Our friend Lazarus has fallen asleep; but I am going there to wake him up' " (verse 11, NIV). And after His wonderful, life-giving prayer, after the miracle, does Lazarus come out of the tomb and give a report of four days in Paradise? Has he been to a homecoming celebration in heaven? If so, he misses a golden opportunity to give Mary and Martha and the news reporters all the details about streets of gold. No, Jesus says very simply: " 'Take off the grave clothes and let him go' " (verse 44, NIV). And it seems clear that Lazarus was simply sleeping, unconscious in the grave, for those four days.

In 1 Thessalonians 4, we find the clearest possible teaching about death and tears. Jesus will come down from heaven with a shout (see verse 16).

That's the Second Coming, of course, a future event. Those who are alive then will rise up, be lifted off this death-scarred old world. But first, the dead in Christ will rise. The dead rise *first*. When? At the Second Coming. All this time they've been sleeping in the grave. And Paul says with absolute clarity that they—and us too—will *meet* the Lord in the air (see verses 16, 17). We've missed each other so much, but now, at long last, we meet. If someone you love has died, the Bible says they will meet Jesus on that wonderful day, the same day you will. Not before. Not at the moment of death. No, we all meet Jesus at the very same moment.

If this scenario is true, what does it mean? It means that when we grieve at funerals because we miss someone, Jesus misses them too! When we cry in our loneliness, He too sheds tears. We're deprived of that laugh, that wonderful friendship, that personality, that loved one—and so is He! He has the same wistfulness we do: the memories, the mementos of happier times gone by, and the intensity of longing for the morning when death will never again hold a loved one.

Is Jesus truly with us in suffering? Does He really relate to our problems? Does He feel the confusion that followed the World Trade Center attack, the numb sense that life will never be bright and happy again? That we will never again feel safe when passing through those X-ray machines at the airport? If you read the great Old Testament statement by God Himself, found in Exodus 34:6, it goes like this: "And He passed in front of Moses, proclaiming, 'The Lord, the Lord, the compassionate and gracious God, slow to anger, abounding in love and faithfulness' " (NIV).

Interesting, and wonderful, isn't it, that the characteristic of compassion is the first thing God tells us about Himself in His divine résumé. He feels with us; He suffers with us. And perhaps it's significant that we find this self-describing word included here at precisely the moment when Moses takes a new set of two stone tablets up to the mountain to replace the ones broken in Israel's earlier rebellion. Does God have compassion even for our sinful state? Does He understand the hard times we have with the devil, the temptations, the moral challenges? Does He understand when you have a hard time telling the truth, when you find it difficult to remain pure in your thoughts and deeds? Does He know the almost painful thirst for revenge that drives a nation that has been attacked, blindsided, by faceless enemies?

There's a marvelous Bible promise about this very truth, found in Hebrews 4:15. Jesus, our Savior, is sympathetic even with the moral failings we experience and struggle with: "We don't have a high priest who doesn't understand us or who's incapable of feeling our pain. He was tempted *more powerfully* than any of us will *ever* be tempted, yet He never sinned or lost His hold on God" (The Clear Word, emphasis supplied).

Maybe you've had the experience of actually weeping over your faults and failures. Satan has just hit you and hit you and hit you until you became hysterical. Well, Jesus has never wept over His failures, because He never failed, but He absolutely has had the experience of having the devil come after Him over and over and over. Matthew 4 tells how Lucifer attacked his enemy three times in a row, in succession—and when Jesus was at His weakest moment: starving and weak and frail.

Does Jesus know harassment? Yes! Does He know relentless temptation? Yes! Does He know what it means to feel beaten down, weighed down, until you almost fall to the ground in discouragement? Yes, He does. It happened to Him in Gethsemane exactly like that. So when you and I cry out, "God, this is hard!" Jesus can relate to it. He can have compassion. Your tears mingle with His.

I had the privilege once of meeting a Hollywood actor named Bruce Marchiano. Bruce, a devout born-again Christian, was called on in 1992, by director Regardt van den Bergh, to play the part of Jesus in a four-hour film based entirely on the book of Matthew. And so this became his immediate challenge: to think—not like some silver-screen villain or a romantic leading man—but to think like *Jesus!* The miraculous, impossible-sounding statement from 1 Corinthians 2:16—"We have the mind of Christ"—was literally his Hollywood assignment.

In his book, *In the Footsteps of Jesus,* Marchiano writes that this was the toughest part of his job. He could bulk up physically with weights so that he looked like a strong thirty-year-old carpenter, an outdoor itinerant preacher. He had a bit of Middle East in his blood already, so the coloring was there. But the *mind* of Christ! How could he accomplish that? "It's essential," he writes in the book, "for an actor to grasp the character's point of view." And, knowledgeable film star that he is, he describes what he calls the "through-line," which is the character's essence and core. What drives this person? What is the main, sometimes mysteriously hidden, foundation conviction that makes this man or woman what he or she is in the deep inside? Everything branches from that "through-line," Bruce explains, and he was determined to find out what that through-line was (p. 115).

As you read through the book, one thing we find is an abundance of tears. Marchiano was always crying. In scene after scene, as they spent literally months in the African desert on location, he would find himself shaking with great sobs. And we wonder, Why?

In the story of the Sheep and the Goats, found in Matthew 25, he had to get himself ready to play out this scene: "When I got to the part, 'Then He will say to those on His left, "Depart from me, you who are cursed, into the eternal fire prepared for the devil and his angels," again a depth of grief enveloped my heart that I can't describe, and I could barely continue with the remainder of the speech. It was like a knife of pain thrust into my heart, and I fought with everything I had to get the final words out. We did two takes on that speech, and on the first I just sat with my back against a wall and cried like a baby. When Regardt finally whispered, 'Cut,' everybody froze—nobody even breathed—and tears were rolling down the cheeks of many crew faces. The cameraman straightened up, his eyes sopping wet, and silently nodded at me over the eyepiece. Everyone was blown away at what had happened—including me."

As Bruce reflects back on the whole experience, two things shine through. He decided, first of all, that the "through-line" of Jesus was this one sentence: "ON A MISSION OF REDEMPTIVE LOVE." That word *love*—defined by redeeming, rescuing, saving, lifting out of slavery, pulling free—that word *love* was the whole essence of Jesus. And he came to realize that 2,000 years ago, Jesus lived among us and basically saw one thing: "A SEA OF PEOPLE LIVING LIVES IN WAYS HE DIDN'T PLAN" (pp. 91, 116).

All around Him were people Jesus loved with such intensity! But time after time, it was His experience to watch in near helplessness as these treasures scurried into sin; they were literally hell-bent on destroying themselves through rebellion. And so when Jesus tells the story of the sheep and the goats—representing people who either live selfless, generous, giving lives, or selfish, egocentric, "me-first" existences—He knew where those "goats" were going to end up. Their selfishness was self-destructive; they were headed into the darkness of their own self-made doom. And this

Hollywood actor, trying so hard to *understand* the despair of Jesus over these wrong paths, these deluded children, just kept bursting into tears.

The sobering reality of this terrorist attack on America is that it was so cold-blooded, so meticulously planned. These "cell groups" had quietly submerged themselves in American communities, living next door to the rest of us. They waited and they planned—and Jesus, looking down, had to watch it all. He had to watch this strategy of terror: the encrypted calls, the surreptitious, coded emails, the satchels of money moving around the nation, buying the tools of terror. People moving away from His divine plan, deluded men departing from the path of peace. All Christ could do was watch and weep.

Earlier in the Matthew story, Marchiano had to do the scene where Jesus cries out: "Woe to you, Korazin! Woe to you, Bethsaida!" (see Matthew 11:21). It's a big crowd scene, with extras milling around, hurrying this way and that, ignoring this bearded Stranger standing among them. Bruce describes them this way: "People living lives away from His love, away from His care; outside of His goodness, His embrace, His plans, purposes, and hopes for them."

Nobody was *doing* anything so wicked or rebellious; they weren't killing or committing rape. They were simply busy, hurrying along, moving *away* from *Him*. And suddenly Bruce saw how that must have seemed to Jesus. All these people, these desperately lonely, sad, busy, confused, lost people running in all directions—except toward Him. And this trained Hollywood professional actor, responded: "It was so awful a thing—I don't have words to describe to you how incredibly awful it was. I remember when it happened, it was as if the wind got knocked out of me; I couldn't breathe, and my heart just *broke*. It broke on a level I never knew existed, and I just started shaking, and weeping . . . I would weep uncontrollably that day for more than an hour, completely unable to compose my emotions" (p. 116).

Well, that wasn't acting. Here we consider two Jesuses, and neither one got an Oscar . . . because they weren't acting. The tears of Jesus are real. When He sees us moving away from Him, living our lives in ways He didn't ever plan, it breaks His heart. And He cries.

What else can we do but to turn around—and to come to Him?

3

Don't Be "Meek," Mr. President!

At least for a while, *Newsweek* magazine stopped giving him "down" arrows in its weekly "Conventional Wisdom" section. *Saturday Night Live*'s Will Farrell had to go on hiatus with his sharp, skewering lampoons of America's forty-third President. Eighty-six percent of all Americans approved of how he was handling the crisis; one hundred senators and 435 representatives were strongly supporting George W. Bush, who went on television a week after the terrorist attacks and flatly stated that America simply was not going to give in, not going to lose this global confrontation.

It's the one character trait no one wants the President of the United States to posses right now: MEEKNESS. No way. The world is looking for a tough, bold, visionary man who can stare down Osama bin Laden and his kind . . . and pulverize them.

With that in mind, is it any great comfort to know that gentle Jesus is in charge of this universe? Can we expect Heaven to react with swift decisiveness and bring an end to the conflagrations that endlessly ruin this troubled world?

What does the dictionary tell us about the term *meek*? Here's the first definition: "Showing patience and humility; gentle." Well, that's all right, although you don't see much of even that on C-SPAN following September 11. But now the second definition: "Easily imposed on; submissive." If accused of being meek, every world leader associated with NATO would immediately call a press conference and issues a denial. "No way! That's not me! I fought in World War II! I stood up to the liberals who wanted to raise your taxes. When I was governor I sent more people to the gas chamber than any other governor. I've been fighting crime in the streets since I was a councilman in Smallville U.S.A. And believe me, I will not rest until these 'cell groups' are hunted down and eradicated." We don't want to be thought of as *meek*.

But doesn't the Bible recommend the quality of meekness? Absolutely! Right in the heart of the Sermon on the Mount and the Beatitudes, Jesus Christ Himself says this: "Blessed are the meek: for they shall inherit the earth" (Matthew 5:5).

So maybe the George Bushes and the Al Gores think to themselves: "Well, I can either be *meek,* or I can be *President.* And if I can't be both, I'd rather be President!" Frankly, when we take the popular notion of meekness, maybe we don't want our presidents to be meek. We want a tough guy in the White House.

This concept of timid, submissive meekness and *weakness* translates directly into our mental picture of Jesus. Haven't we all prayed: "Gentle Jesus, meek and mild, look upon this little child"? In these days, as we watch crews valiantly trying to clean up the mountains of rubble in New York City, we'd much prefer: "*Mighty* Jesus, great and strong, beat my enemies all day long!" The world applauded the courageous passengers aboard United Airlines Flight 93 who didn't meekly accept their fate, but instead rushed the cockpit and downed the plane in a barren field, sparing more innocent lives.

Frequently art museums and cathedrals contain paintings of Jesus in which He certainly does look meek. The Savior looks pale and timid. When I preach using PowerPoint® illustrations, I search vainly on my clip-art CDs for a picture in which Jesus looks fit and muscular like home-run slugger Mark McGwire; most of the time the crucified Lord looks more like the batboy—and I say that reverently. On the cross, Jesus is depicted as weighing a mere 98 pounds. Standing there in front of the Roman soldiers, He simply takes whatever they dish out.

And of course, some passages of Scripture do support our conception of meekness as weakness. In Matthew 11:29, Christ says about Himself: "Take my yoke upon you, and learn of me; for I am meek and lowly in heart."

When we consider *meek* to mean "easily imposed on or submissive"— do we discover Jesus there? Yes, frankly, we do. Jesus *was* imposed on; He stood in Pilate's hall and took that beating. People who wanted to be healed, who needed miracles imposed themselves on Christ. He turned the other cheek; He submitted to the cross, Paul says in Philippians 2:8.

So what do Christians do with this biblical command for *us* to be meek? How can we get the promised blessing without surrendering our wills and our intestinal fortitude and having the Osama bin Ladens of the world walk right over us to get to our wallets or take away our security?

The *NIV Study Bible* contains an interesting text note right under the "meek" beatitude found in Matthew 5:5: "This beatitude refers not so much to an attitude toward *man* as to a disposition before *God*, namely, humility."

Regardless of how we feel we ought to relate to other people, do you agree that meekness before God is absolutely proper? We want to submit before Him; we want to have God impose *His* will upon us. To adopt a get-tough, presidential-candidate attitude before the God of the universe would be the most foolish thing a human being could ever do. No, a humble, self-effacing spirit is a correct attitude to have when you're kneeling before Heaven's throne.

But that still leaves the question about how to deal with each other. Do we want to be meek with our spouses and our friends . . . and people who intended to do us violence? If you looked in a thesaurus under the word *Christian*, will you find *doormat* listed as a synonym?

I love stories in which men and women, Bible champions, are so secure in God that they *know* in their hearts a kind of special strength. They're not cocky; they're not blustering and boastful and throwing their accomplishments in your face. In fact, if you looked at them, they might appear humble and meek. But under the surface is a power that's not *their* power. It's power from a heavenly source.

I heard an old story once of a Quaker who was deeply religious. And of course, he was nonviolent, a pacifist, soft-spoken, very humble. You'd think he'd be the biggest pushover on the block. Apparently, a certain burglar decided that too. And one night at about 2:00 A.M., this quiet Quaker heard noises from downstairs. A little bit of rustling and commotion and jingling of silver as the family treasures were being stuffed into a bag.

This Quaker crept down to the landing on the stairs. There in the moonlight he could clearly see the burglar going about his business. And there was a very ominous clicking sound as this quiet Quaker cocked both barrels of a shotgun. And then he said quietly, "Friend, I would not hurt thee for the world. *(Pause)* But thee is standing where I am about to shoot."

Now here was a man who was MEEK! But he had a big gun. He had a close relationship with another power, a power named Smith & Wesson, with the ability to protect and defend. And in the safety of that relationship, this very meek man was also very safe. He had a rare strength *in* his meekness.

In Psalm 76:7-9, there's a picture of people who benefit from their connection with a mighty God: "Thou, even thou [God], art to be feared: and who may stand in thy sight when once thou art angry? Thou didst cause judgment to be heard from heaven; the earth feared, and was still, when God arose to judgment, to save all the meek of the earth."

If we're right with God, we can know that *He will save*—and that *we* can then be meek, humble and gentle with those around us. We don't have to fight them; God will do that for us.

There's a wonderful picture of Christlike meekness found in the classic old story *Ben-Hur: A Tale of the Christ.* Hidden in the filmed dramatization is an almost perfect illustration of the kind of meekness Jesus had.

The director never allows us to see Jesus Himself on the screen. All through the film there are only hints of the Savior. When Judah Ben-Hur is being led through the desert with the other criminals on their way to serve as galley slaves, there's a scene where they all stop to rest. And inside a carpenter shop, we glimpse a strong arm holding a tool. That's all—just a strong arm. A *hint* of a young Man named Jesus of Nazareth.

And then comes The Moment. Judah has collapsed in the dirt. He's exhausted, both physically and spiritually. Will he ever see his family again? Will he even survive this horrible journey? Will he die at sea, chained to an oar as the Roman galley sinks beneath the waves? As he claws for a drink of water, just a sip being provided by the kind Jewish woman, the Roman commandant blusters at her: "No water for him! No water for him!"

Scared and trembling, she reluctantly obeys. Judah Ben-Hur gets no water. And now this slave is in complete despair. He falls prostrate on the ground, sobbing. "Oh, God, help me!" Is life going to end right there?

Suddenly there's a strong hand lifting his head. A strong hand brushes away the dirt and gives him a long drink of water. We only see the hand, but we know who it belongs to. And Judah looks up in wonderment at that face, that face we can't see. Who is this mysterious Man who has given him water?

Suddenly the Roman officer looks over. What! Someone dares to give this prisoner a drink? Against his direct orders? What's going on here? "Hey!" he barks out, ready to assert his authority again. "I said no water for him!" He takes a step forward, girding up his loins for a confrontation.

And then, in a beautiful cinematic moment, this mysterious Man slowly stands up. We see Him only from the back, but as He stands to His feet, with Judah Ben-Hur resting in His shadow, He seems to grow and expand in quiet strength. How tall *is* this Man? He dwarfs the Roman officer, who suddenly stops in his tracks.

And there's that long moment. Jesus Christ, Defender of the weak and the dying and even the thirsty prisoner, doesn't say a word. We don't see His face. We don't hear any thunder. But somehow this divine Man has something inside of Him that asserts its raw power. And the Roman officer kind of blinks, chews on his lip for a nervous moment, and then backs away. All in dead silence, he backs away.

Why is this scene such a powerful picture of *good* meekness? First of all, it epitomizes the very *quiet strength* we crave right now. Jesus Christ, without saying a word, simply stands tall, a Mount Everest—and His enemies retreat.

But the second point is even more stirring. The meekness of Jesus means that He is strong to defend others, not strong to defend Himself. And that's actually the Bible picture of meekness. Strong and firm and unmovable in the defense of other people, instead of strong and firm and unmovable in the defense of ourselves.

Over and over again, Jesus was strong in defending the weak. He looked daggers at a man or woman who would cause another person, perhaps a child, to fall into sin. He was strong to look the Pharisees and Sadducees in the eye and describe how their sins were leading the entire nation to ruin. He towered over that Roman officer who was keeping Judah Ben-Hur from those few drops of water.

But when the opportunity came to defend Himself there in Pilate's court, Christ was meek. "He never said a mumblin' word," the old spiritual tells us.

Maybe soldiers understand this concept of meekness more easily than the rest of us. They fight more to protect others than to protect themselves. They fight for their spouses and children and aged parents back home. They fight to defend the person in the trench next to them; if there's a bullet to be taken, they take it so someone else can live.

But where did this one-of-a-kind Man, Jesus Christ, get His inner strength? We sometimes find quiet, underlying strength in the most unpredictable places. Someone you might think epitomizes the "wimpy" image of meekness is actually as tough as nails.

I once spent the summer working at a retirement center in St. Helena, California, and it was my daily assignment to drive the senior citizens into town to run their errands. I remember seeing a little old man, ninety years old, using a walker to slowly make his way down the hallway toward the van. And immediately my mind reacted: "Poor guy, trying to get along like that. All the muscles aren't what they used to be. I guess I'll pray for him."

But then I took Mr. Jones's hand to help him aboard. *Yow!* The guy's grip nearly shattered all the bones in my hand! This man had a grip that would bend steel!

Now, his bent-over, 140-pound frame didn't look that strong. His legs were obviously weakened, so I assumed he was weak—and *meek*—all over. But because of those frail legs, he had to use the walker to maneuver up and down those hallways, up and down stairs, over to the dining room, out to the parking lot. And so his arms, and especially his *grip,* was powerful! If it came down to arm wrestling, old Mr. Jones could have cleaned my clock right-handed and left-handed!

Jesus illustrates that very same point. He got so much spiritual exercise, studying God's Word and spending long hours in prayer, that His relationship with His heavenly Father was almost like a dependence on a walker. And it built Him up! Despite His demeanor of peacefulness and humility *and meekness,* Jesus Christ had inner strength. He had a spiritual grip that was made of iron. When it came down to the Thursday evening when the Roman soldiers tied His arms, Jesus didn't look very strong. But inside where it counted, the Savior of our world had built up muscles that would see Him through the horrors of Calvary.

In Galatians 5, where Paul lists the fruits of the spirit, meekness is mentioned in the same breath as peace, patience, goodness, faithfulness, and self-control. Those are all strong, muscular words. Perhaps you've never thought of them in that way. But it's the strong who champion peace; the weak give in to the temptation to fight and squabble and throw stones and carpet-bomb their enemy's entire country. It's the strong who are faithful; it's the strong who exhibit self-control; it's the strong who patiently and carefully assemble a global coalition to stand against tyranny. It is the weak who have the temper tantrums and the intemperate binges.

In the film *Witness,* writers Earl Wallace and William Kelley describe a scene in which a New York City policeman is hiding in the Pennsylvania Amish country from a rogue police captain who is illicitly involved in a huge drug deal. John Book has been wounded in his attempt to uncover the evil story, and for several weeks, the peace-loving Amish people, with their quiet ways and their plain black clothing, have nursed him back to health.

Of course the Amish are dedicated to complete nonviolence. More than perhaps any other group, they "turn the other cheek." Toward the end of the story, though, the noose begins to tighten. The crooked police captain from New York finally tracks down his adversary. And he drives to this little community, determined to kill the one man who knows the truth. There's something very wrenching about the specter of violence in such a peaceful, idyllic setting. It appears that the drug-dealing police captain is going to triumph. He has John Book in his gunsight, and there's no one to stop him.

And then an Amish bell begins to ring. Over and over this bell clangs out a message that farmers all through the area recognize. "Drop what you're doing and come. Quickly!" And from all the surrounding farms and fields, these quiet, strong Amish men begin to appear. Some hold pitchforks and hoes; none of them have guns. But a good thirty or forty of them are suddenly on the premises. And they quietly surround this criminal with his *one* gun.

And he suddenly realizes that he can't win. He can't triumph against all of them. Yes, he could shoot one or two. But he can't kill them all. Even though he's in the midst of absolute *meekness* and passivity, he can't win. The unity of these soft-spoken bearded men, standing there wordlessly in their black overalls and plain straw hats . . . that unity is an awesome weapon, a fortress against his evil and his one puny little gun.

It's a beautiful moment when John Book says to him, "You have to give up. It's over." And slowly the gun comes down. The police captain drops it in the dirt and submits to arrest, to the raw power of meekness.

Meekness is strength when many godly people come together. Submission and humility and even "turning the other cheek" become weapons when we stand shoulder to shoulder with the rest of the army of Jesus Christ. In Matthew 18:20 Jesus reminds us of this very fact: "Where two or three are gathered together in my name, there am I in the midst of them."

Prayer is a form of worship that may not seem very tough. People on their knees with their eyes closed talking to a Deity they can't see—that's the very picture of meekness, isn't it? And how is it that two people praying together are a more potent force than just one? I don't have the answer to that question—but the Bible says it's true. When a group of people pray, they become an army. A meek army, to be sure. They're on their knees, which is the classic pose of surrender. But when many people pray together, the devil with his one rusty little shotgun has no choice but to give in.

Here's another way of highlighting that same point. I'm just one Christian, one pastor, receiving the same salary as every other minister in my Adventist denomination. What I put in the plate each week for tithes and offerings can't really do that much. It's a few thousand dollars a year . . . and I'm glad to give it.

But when you combine that with the sacrificial giving of *twelve million* Seventh-day Adventists around the globe, and the billions that are given to the Lord by my Baptist friends and my Presbyterian brothers and sisters, then HUGE things are accomplished. I've seen them. New missions are established; Christian hospitals heal and save countless lives; Bible schools—elementary, high school, colleges, universities—train millions to love and serve the Lord. All because we quietly and humbly give together.

Right after those two huge skyscrapers in New York City came crashing down, people began to get out their wallets. Just a few days later, every competing network in America offered to share and carry the same "feed," to broadcast the same two-hour telethon concert. How often does that happen? But "where two or three are gathered . . ." Millions of people watching got out their VISA cards and called toll-free numbers. Fifty bucks here. A hundred. Ten. Five. Together, it added up to hundreds of millions.

There's a second definition to this elusive word *meek* to be considered. Back in 1988 presidential candidate Michael Dukakis essentially lost the election when a reporter asked him in a televised debate: "What would you say or do, Governor Dukakis, if somebody raped and killed your wife? Are you for executions or what?" And Dukakis, all five feet six inches of him, timidly replied: "Well, you know, I'm not in favor of the death penalty. And I guess I would, uh . . . uh . . ." *Turn out the lights; the election's over.*

Here's the point: biblical meekness can mean that we are *always* angry at the right time, *never* angry at the wrong time.

The assignment to write radio sermons commemorating Martin Luther King, Jr.'s birthday made me aware of a young Christian minister who got angry at the right times. No, he wasn't a perfect human being; he made mistakes. But his life showed a pattern of becoming angry about things that *should* make a Christian angry. Racism made him angry. Injustice and lost opportunities and wasted human potential made him angry. Unreasonable slowness in the struggle for civil rights made him angry. Laziness and apathy and reverse racism often brought him to despair.

Jesus was One whose anger was rare. But it was there. At the right time, it was there . . . and it was something to see. That's the *good* anger, the good and timely indignation of our holy Savior and Lord. He was angry on September 11 as He watched His children die. As President Bush said in that eloquent speech nine days later—as crafted by born-again Christian speechwriter Michael Gerson: "Freedom and fear, justice and cruelty, have always been at war, and we know that God is not neutral between them."

But Jesus was never angry at the wrong time. In Luke 9 we read about indignation that His disciples felt. After an unsuccessful witnessing trip to a certain Samaritan village, the twelve fledgling preachers were disgusted: "Lord, do You want us to call fire down from heaven to destroy them?"

Their feelings were hurt. They'd been rejected, and they didn't like it. They were feeling anger for their own sake. Actually, if anyone had cause to feel personal resentment, it was Christ. After all, it was His message these people had scorned. But what did Jesus do? He rebuked His disciples: " 'You do not know what manner of spirit you are of. For the Son of Man did not come to destroy men's lives but to save them' " (verses 55, 56, NKJV).

That's quite a picture, isn't it? *Meekness*—angry at the right time, never at the wrong time. How can we walk this tightrope of *proper* anger? How can we learn to not be angry at the wrong times? How can we know what the wrong times are?

Again, our Example's name is Jesus Christ. And we see several powerful weapons that He used in His own human struggle against inappropriate anger.

Prayer is one. Christ prayed incessantly. He prayed before those three wilderness temptations. He prayed all night before being hounded the next day by sick people and hypocritical church leaders and dumb, pride-filled disciples. He prayed in the Garden of Gethsemane for sure—knowing that the next day was going to bring hard-pounding rage temptations that would be almost humanly impossible to resist.

Here's another biblical hint. We need to fortify our minds with Scripture and the pillars of Christian truth. Let's say you have a moment of real emotional tension with your spouse. You arrive home late for supper, and so you have a vicious argument. Both of you are already angry, and you're tempted to nurture that anger, to hang on to it, and let it grow. But you're reminded that, as Christians, you have an obligation to forgive each other. The Bible teaches that! You *know* it! What's more, we're instructed as believers to forgive each other *now, today!* Don't let the sun go down on your anger, the Bible says (see Ephesians 4:26).

If we have biblical principles in our minds and Scripture verses written in our hearts, we're going to have a huge advantage in the fight against improper anger! True, we'll still flare up; we'll have moments when a quick flame ignites. That's part of having a sinful human nature—and we can be thankful for God's patience with us as the life-long process of sanctification continues. But a Christian who accepts Bible truth and feeds regularly on it will have a very real and tangible safeguard; he or she can really grow to be MEEK.

And a third reality—we need the Holy Spirit too. We need His guidance. To know when to fight and when to lay back. When to defend and when to surrender our claims.

The most important question, certainly, is this: In the end, what will happen to the meek people? We know what it says in the Beatitudes, but really—what will happen?

A timid man was sitting at the counter of an interstate truck stop, quietly drinking his cocoa, when ten members of a motorcycle gang walked in. And for some reason they decided to pick on this less-than-muscular fellow. They edged up against him, bumping him and knocking over his drink, picking french fries off his plate, and, in general, giving him quite a bit of abuse. And he didn't say a word of protest; of course, it *was* ten against one—and they had a lot more tattoos than he did. Finally he slipped through the crowd and went over to the cash register. He didn't complain or demand a refund for all the cocoa he didn't drink. He simply paid his bill and left.

One biker even began to boast to the cashier. "I guess we showed him. Poor baby's probably gone off to cry to his mama."

And another one said, "Huh! Not much of a man. He didn't fight back or nothin'!"

The cashier glanced out the window and then said, "You know, he's not much of a truck driver either. He just ran his eighteen-wheeler right over ten motorcycles out there."

Is this biblical meekness? Letting people steal your fries and knock over your cup of cocoa, and then plotting a later revenge? Are we meek in the restaurant and a tiger behind the wheel of a Peterbilt truck, ready to run right over bin Laden and his associates?

Consider just once more what exactly Jesus said there on the mount: "Blessed are the meek: for they shall inherit the earth."

So these people receive God's blessing. They live under the umbrella of blessing, the security of knowing they're in the center of God's will.

Here's something else. The meek *will* inherit the earth. We could explore all sorts of interpretations of that: are God's people going to take over and live in the White House and at Number 10 Downing Street? Is there a biblical guarantee that the United States and its allies can oust the Taliban and establish a fair and tolerant government in Afghanistan? The Bible doesn't give that specific promise, but we can know for sure that those who are spiritually meek *aren't* going to end up empty-handed.

Our friend in the truck stop had his French fries taken; the bikers tipped over his cocoa and stole his lunch. But according to the Bible's promise, a person who responds with meekness will not end up with nothing in the end.

Now, the trucker left the diner hungry *that afternoon*. Sometimes there is a temporary time of deprivation. A spirit of meekness and humility may get your paycheck stolen, your groceries ripped off, your reputation stained. In the short term, God's humble people get the short end of some bargains. They get sued and sometimes they don't sue back, in accordance with 1 Corinthians 6. But Matthew 5 gives assurance that when in the big picture, the meek won't be left empty-handed. They'll have their hands full with the blessings of God; they'll inherit the earth.

Interestingly, Jesus was quoting from the Old Testament when He gave that particular part of the Sermon on the Mount. In Psalm 37:11 we read that "the meek will inherit the land and enjoy great peace" (NIV). This is actually a double blessing! Not only do these special people inherit the land and have their hands full of God's blessings, but they enjoy peace. An abundance of peace. That means those ten husky bikers will be gone! They won't be harassing you any longer. Those who "lay back" and trust in God for protection will come to a time when there will be peace. Their enemies will be removed from the scene; those who ripped them off won't be on the plantation any longer.

It's thrilling news that the idea of meekness is coupled with following God, linking up with Him, allying yourself with Him.

Zephaniah 3:12 says: " 'But I will leave within you the meek and humble, who trust in the name of the Lord' " (NIV). Meekness and being in relationship with God are twin concepts that *have* to go together. In a way, I agree with the world's view and the current "Bush Doctrine" that meekness *in and of itself* is something to be avoided. To just sit there and take slap after slap in the face, bomb after bomb, atrocity after atrocity, affront after affront—without holding on to that larger view of God and His willingness to defend and His ultimate plan for you—*is* an unwholesome thing.

But what a difference when Christians ride out storm after storm, knowing that their lives are in the hands of Someone who is stronger than any storm, mightier than any wave. Maybe we can even more appreciate the biblical challenge to meekness when we read and reread this promise in Isaiah 49:25: " 'I will contend with those who contend with you' " (NIV).

"Your enemies will become *My* enemies," God promises. But it's hard sometimes to be patient and to wait for that day when the promises of Isaiah 49 and Matthew 5 are to be fulfilled. There seems to be such a long delay, while the meek walk around with empty pockets and bruises and empty dinner plates. And during times like those, we have to keep asking ourselves: Am I willing to trust God in the darkness? Am I willing to wait?

In *Disappointment With God,* Philip Yancey takes a wonderfully challenging look at the dilemma of waiting! Job had to wait. Many of God's champions lay down for the last time, having received *none* of the rewards promised. Their own bin Ladens were alive and well, still terrorizing them. The Promised Land was still a long way off (p. 197).

Yancey writes about how two great Jewish writers, Jerzy Kozinski and Elie Wiesel "began with a strong faith in God, but saw it vaporize in the gas furnaces of the Holocaust. Face to face with history's grossest unfairness, they concluded that God must not exist" (p. 207).

What's the answer? Yancey's answer runs 314 pages, but in the final analysis, he believes God can be trusted. God *will* contend with those who contend with us. *In the end,* He will do what He says He will do. The meek will be blessed; they will inherit the earth; they will know that their enemies are gone. "We are given few details about that future world," Yancey writes, "only a promise that God will prove Himself trustworthy" (p. 299).

Our decision about meekness boils down to this. We can fight for ourselves, or we can let God fight for us. Which of those two do we want?

4

How Mad Is God Right About Now?

What is the *angriest* you have ever been? Do you remember? Was it on September 11, 2001? That came real close for me; I don't mind confessing it.

It's probably easiest to remember the person who was the object of your rage. But do you recall your feelings that day? Did you get to the point where you were actually shaking with anger? Red in the face? Fists clenched? Obscenities and curse words screaming in your head? If you were Ted Olson, our U.S. Solicitor General, whose wife, Barbara, was on the plane that smashed into the Pentagon, wouldn't you feel that way about Khalid Al-Midhar, Majed Moqed, Nawaq Alhazmi, Salem Alhazmi, and Hani Hanjour?

In this dark moment in our planet's history, we naturally think about the anger of God—what the Bible calls the "wrath of God." Any other time, this would not be a popular topic. What does it mean when we read that God gets angry? Does He have fists that He can clench? Are there veins in the neck of the Almighty Father that stand out when the children of Israel bow down to false gods? In this decadent, selfish new millennium, does He get purple in the face when people commit murders or when He hears what's going out on rap CDs or playing on network television? Did

He fume as He watched American Airlines Flight 77 plow resolutely into that stately, five-sided building in our nation's capital?

It's not an oxymoron—especially not just now—when we talk about the *good* temper of God. There is such a thing as the wrath of God, the anger of our heavenly Father. And it's a good kind of anger.

It's good news, as we watch our television sets, that it's possible to have anger and still not sin. Ephesians 4:26 says very clearly, "In your anger do not sin" (NIV). And the *NIV Study Bible* text note says: "Christians do not lose their emotions at conversion, but their emotions should be purified. Some anger is sinful, some is not."

Clearly God's anger is of the appropriate kind. His anger is a good anger, but what does that mean? What makes His anger righteous instead of stained with unholy thoughts and mean selfishness and revenge like ours?

Exodus 34:6, 7 contains this clear statement from God Himself: " 'The Lord, the Lord, the compassionate and gracious God, slow to anger, abounding in love and faithfulness, maintaining love to thousands, and forgiving wickedness, rebellion and sin' " (NIV).

So God can get angry; and yes, He does get angry. But it's an anger that comes slowly; it develops in a controlled way and for good reasons. There's no sudden, volatile eruption of rage, no temper tantrums with God. God always gets angry for a good reason.

What would you think of a United States President who was not only slow to anger, but who never did get angry? A man with no temper capacity whatsoever?

Imagine the scene. Aides rush to his side: "Mr. President, planes just crashed into the World Trade Center. Thousands are dead."

And he looks at them. "So? What's that got to do with me? I'm safe and sound at Emma E. Booker Elementary School. They're not going to attack us here in Saratoga, Florida."

"Well, aren't we going to do something?"

And he looks at his appointment schedule and then says: "Well, see if the FBI can look into it. Put Cheney on it. I'm going to Disney World."

Or it comes in over the wire that millions are starving to death in Rwanda. They're being massacred in Bosnia. And the president says: "Who cares? It's not *my* problem. Call the Red Cross or something." Unemployment jumps up two points and millions of real people lose their jobs, but the president looks at poll numbers and says: "I can still win reelection. Big deal." Or let's say that enemy planes bomb Pearl Harbor and F. D. R. just gives a shrug and pats Fala on the head: "Oh well. At least I wasn't there. What's for lunch?"

No! We *want* a President who can get angry at the right time and in the right way. A president who can say to the workers in the ruins: "I hear you. And soon the people who did this are going to hear you!" What do we consider to maybe be Franklin Roosevelt's finest hour, his best sound bite? Of course: "December seventh, 1941. A date which will live in infamy." Roosevelt was angry; he was righteously angry, and we were glad for his quiet, controlled rage. We applauded when President George Bush, Sr., a decade ago, responded to Saddam Hussein's encroachment on a helpless neighbor. "This shall not stand," he said. And that was good anger.

There are limits, certainly, to what good anger can accomplish. But one thing is so often true. Frequently, nothing happens until someone gets angry. A change doesn't take place until someone's temper begins to boil in the right way. As Peter Finch said in the film *Network,* "First, you've got to get mad."

God looks down at this planet, and He sees many things that make Him angry. He'd be a terrible God if He *didn't* get angry. He'd be an unfeeling, impotent, useless deity if what happened on September 11, 2001, didn't make Him angry. Thank God His anger has moved Him to action. God got angry enough to step in and begin clearing away the rubble and to start rebuilding lives.

A news story came along a few years ago that was so painfully strange, so offbeat, that I hesitate to even mention it. But in the skimpiest of details, a school teacher, a high school athletic coach, was arrested, along with his wife, for the crime of enticing male students to be with his wife. I'll just leave it at that.

Now why? Who can understand the mentality of such a couple? To recruit other people, and especially kids, to take your own wife—it runs so contrary to human instinct, and especially a male human's instinct, that about all we can do is to shake our heads. There's no good explanation for it, and I confess that I didn't even try to follow the unfolding stories in the paper to discover what this couple's *bad* explanation might be.

There *ought* to beat in the heart of any good man a kind of good jealousy. There is a jealousy that is appropriate and holy and wholesome. A normal man, and especially a Christian man, has a God-given instinct to protect his spouse from the advances of any other man. I can state categorically that if someone attempts to mess with my wife, Lisa Jean Smith, that person *will* find themselves dealing with me. That's not macho bravado or hot air or a bit of frustrated Arnold Schwarzenegger talk. That's God's intention for Christian couples. We ought to be jealous for one another. Protective. Wanting your spouse's affections all to yourself. Text notes for Exodus 20:5 *(NIV Study Bible)* give this explanation: "God will not put up with rivalry or unfaithfulness. . . . Actually, jealousy is part of the vocabulary of love. The 'jealousy' of God demands exclusive devotion to Himself and delivers to judgment all who oppose Him."

We can be glad He gets angry when someone tries to steal us away. Glad for His holy rage when we're lied to, when our children are abused, when a false picture of Him is left on our doorstep or comes to our mailbox. Can we find a picture of God emerging from these positive benefits of good anger?

First of all, *anger makes people listen.* We notice that in the workplace. And in memories of our third-grade classroom where the teacher expressed a good anger. "Billy, you stop that right now! You're not going to bully little David anymore!" Sometimes a raised voice, raised in a controlled way, can be a powerful weapon for the cause of righteousness.

One of the most unusual paintings I remember illustrated a story in the classic Arthur Maxwell books entitled *The Bible Story.* Perhaps you recall that ten-volume series with their blue covers and the marvelous stories that took us kids right from Genesis through to Revelation. But in volume nine, about the life of Christ, is a picture of an angry Jesus driving out the moneychangers. He's got that little whip in His hand, and praise God, He's mad! One Bible commentary describes the scene this way: "His voice sounded like a trumpet through the temple. The displeasure of His countenance seemed like consuming fire. With authority He commanded, 'Take these things hence' " (*The Desire of Ages,* p. 591).

Here's Benefit Number Two. *Good anger often fuels a movement.*

The civil rights movement is a good example. The rage of an Abraham Lincoln who watched slaves being sold in the marketplace, where he clenched his fists and said to himself, so the story goes, "If I ever get a chance to hit that thing, I'll hit it hard!" Or Gandhi and the controlled anger that was the hallmark of his crusade of nonviolent protest. And now in the wake of those terrorist attacks there are many quiet, wise people who recognize that evil must be met with resolute strength. "Our war on terror," President Bush said, "begins with Al Qaeda, but it does not end there. It will not end until every terrorist group of global reach has been found, stopped, and defeated."

It was God's anger against sin itself that fueled the greatest movement of all human history: the saga of Calvary. The Cross is God's expression against evil and death; it's a campaign *driven* by our heavenly Father's good rage against what we've all been through in this one sin-stained corner of His universe.

C. S. Lewis writes in *Mere Christianity*: "Enemy-occupied territory— that is what this world is. Christianity is the story of how the rightful king had landed, you might say landed in disguise, and is calling us all to take part in a great campaign of sabotage" (p. 51). And it's God's good anger that fuels this war.

Benefit Number Three: *Anger defends the weak*. God says very sternly to some sinners: " 'If anyone causes one of these little ones who believe in me to sin, it would be better for him to have a large millstone hung around his neck and to be drowned in the depths of the sea' " (Matthew 18:6, NIV).

What a beautiful thing to read how God's anger is especially expressed in defense of children! Juliana McCourt, four years old, was on American Airlines Flight 11, on her way to Disneyland with her mom, Ruth. And God is angry over the blind, evil injustice of it all.

Benefit Number Four is that *anger gives a person strength*. All through the Bible, God's actions seem to define the military motto "Peace Through Strength." God's anger against corruption, against sin, against death camps, against satanic selfishness, against faceless terrorist cell groups all give Him the incredible strength to move, to act.

And yet one more benefit: *God's good anger speaks out to defend His own name*.

Statesmen debate whether America should use the term *war* in describing the ordeal that lies ahead. But consider that God doesn't need to defend territory or forts or really even armies of angels. It's not that kind of a war at all. If it were simply a case of who kills the most enemies, God could win in a heartbeat. But this is a war concerning His reputation. And I thrill when I read Bible stories in which God moves with holy indignation to defend His own name. In 1 Samuel 12:22, the prophet says: " 'For the sake of his great name the Lord will not reject his people, because the Lord was pleased to make you his own' " (NIV).

In Psalm 106 is a sad reminder of the human race's sins and rebellions. But then in verse 8 comes this astonishing statement about God's response: "Yet He saved them for His name's sake, to make His mighty power known" (NIV).

Those of us who stand in pulpits every weekend need to fall to our knees during the six days of preparation. We're talking about God! Taking Bible verses and interpreting them. Painting word pictures of a holy God in heaven. What if we mess up? What if our pictures are incorrect and unscriptural? What if we stain God's name instead of uplifting it? Speaking for myself and for my brothers and sisters who are people of the cloth, God's holy reputation is very precious to us, and we don't want to have any part in causing damage to His name.

Whenever we're tempted to hate *people* and vent our anger, it would be well to remember that it is sin we should really hate. After the World Trade Center attacks, *Newsweek's* respected columnist Fareed Zakaria pointed out that "not a single Afghan has been directly tied to any terrorist attack against the West" (Oct. 1, 2001, p. 34). Were you tempted to paint a sign instructing Bush to bomb Afghanistan to smithereens? And take out a few million Afghans with some smart bombs? That's the wrong target, says Zakaria. He continues: "This is a vast Arab operation *that happens to be based in Afghanistan.*" How easy it is for us to hate the first convenient scapegoat we can find!

All of this takes us to a thought that is both very real and very thrilling. What is it that makes God angry? What is it that stirs His passions? We see the clearest glimpses of it whenever His children are harmed. When sin hurts sinners, God's temper is seen. When the innocent are spoiled, when the helpless are abused, when people who want to do right are pushed and shoved and pummeled —that makes God angry with a good anger.

God also demonstrates His rage when someone *could* be reached with the news of salvation—and then is passed by. When someone could be saved, but isn't—that, more than anything else in this universe, causes a righteous ache, a good anger in the heart of God.

Imagine the scenario that comes from a thousand network television movies. Your child is lost or kidnapped or dying of a fatal disease. And someone out there could help him or her—and they fail to. Someone sees your little girl in a bus depot, but doesn't bother to call the police. They see her picture on their milk carton. "Wait a minute," they wonder. "Wasn't that her I saw yesterday at that restaurant? Sure looks like her." But they're watching *Who Wants to Be a Millionaire?* and by the time Regis says goodbye, they forget to dial the toll-free number. Or some medical clinic has the cure for what your precious little baby boy is dying from—but won't release it because you haven't got the money to pay.

What kind of anger do you feel then?

In *The Desire of Ages,* Ellen White describes the similar reaction of God. "Divine love has been stirred to its infathomable depths for the sake of men," she writes, "and angels marvel to behold in the recipients of so great love a mere surface gratitude. Angels marvel at man's shallow appreciation for the love of God. Heaven stands indignant at the neglect shown to the souls of men. Would we know how Christ regards it? How would a father and mother feel, did they know that their child, lost in the cold and the snow, had been passed by, and left to perish, *by those who might have saved it?* Would they not be terribly grieved, wildly indignant? Would they not denounce those murderers with wrath hot as their tears, intense as their love? The sufferings of every man are the sufferings of God's child, and those who reach out no helping hand to their perishing fellow beings provoke His righteous anger."

Then the writer adds this clear indictment: "This is the wrath of the Lamb. To those who claim fellowship with Christ, yet have been indifferent to the needs of their fellow men, He will declare in the great Judgment day, 'I know you not whence ye are; depart from Me, all ye workers of iniquity' " (page 825, emphasis supplied).

It's hard for us to picture the wild indignation of a God who weeps as we continually pass by the opportunities to save our brother and sister. A God whose anger matches His incomparable love. And it's always an anger that's controlled and quietly effective. So often our anger is volatile and *un*controlled because it's a helpless anger. We're shouting into the wind, and we know we can't win. Our boss isn't going to change his mind; our spouse isn't going to change his or her ways. We can't go running blindly out into the Afghan desert all by ourselves and drag terrorists in for questioning. So we're helplessly mad.

But isn't it wonderful, in contrast to that, to see our heavenly Father swing into *effective* action? His anger works; it's controlled and appropriately deadly. It destroys what needs destroying, but saves every single thing and person it possibly can.

One last question, though, must be asked. Will the war ever end? Does even God feel the impotence, the helplessness, of facing an enemy who can't be defeated? As America weighed its response to bin Laden's unsigned assault, Secretary Rumsfeld warned the nation that this would not be a war with a clean, final ending. "You're not going to see a surrender signing on the deck of the *U.S.S. Missouri*," he pointed out.

As we look to our White House and to our men and women in Congress, and as Canadians look to Parliament, and our British allies turn to Tony Blair, we sense the helplessness. Wars and skirmishes flash all around the globe, and our leaders simply don't know how to bring them to an honorable conclusion—or really to any conclusion. "We will not tire," President Bush promised us. "We will not falter, and we will not fail." Every politician promises peace, but they really don't know how to deliver it.

What does this have to do with the good anger of God?

In Matthew 13, Jesus told a parable that gives us a picture of the power of God *and* of His good anger. " 'The kingdom of heaven is like a man who sowed good seed in his field,' " He told them. " 'But while everyone was sleeping, his enemy came and sowed weeds among the wheat, and went away. When the wheat sprouted and formed heads, then the weeds also appeared. The owner's servants came to him and said, "Sir, didn't you sow good seed in your field? Where then did the weeds come from?" "An enemy did this," he replied. The servants asked him, "Do you want us to go and pull them up?" "No," he answered, "because while you are pulling the weeds, you may root up the wheat with them. Let both grow together until the harvest." ' " (verses 24-30, NIV).

If this Bible story stopped right at that point, we would have cause for discouragement. We're surrounded by evil today; the scars of sin are everywhere. Along with that landowner, we look out at all the cemeteries and broken homes and wars and stock market fraud and shattered dreams and that enormous crater where architect Minoru Yamasaki's glorious twin towers used to stand above the Manhattan skyline, and we can't help but say again, "An enemy did this. Someone named Lucifer came through here last Tuesday morning."

And God's people cry out to heaven and say, "Lord, get rid of these weeds! Pull them out. Take Osama bin Laden out back and shoot him! Obliterate every cell in his body, and every cell group he has fomented!" And in this story, it sounds like God just sits back and says, "No, let the weeds stay. Let the weeds and the wheat grow together until the harvest." In other words, sin is going to stay with us for a while. The misery is going to continue. There will be other attacks and other mass graves and more presidential statements in the National Cathedral.

Fortunately, there is more to the parable. This is the rest of the story: " 'At that time,' " Jesus says in describing the harvest, " 'I will tell the harvesters: First collect the weeds and tie them in bundles to be burned; then gather the wheat and bring it into my barn" ' " (NIV).

And in that cryptic story we find a picture of a God who does indeed plan to *solve* the sin problem. What's going on now isn't going to go on forever. Not because NATO is so resolute and our Congress is so smart, but because God has a plan to bring sin to a final and complete end. The stain of sin is going to be forever removed from God's universe.

Please don't misunderstand. I'm not eager for sinners to be punished, and neither should you be. But for the grace of God and the story of Calvary, we'd all be included in that number. But we can appreciate the clear theme running through all sixty-six books of the Bible that tells us God does have a plan to bring sin to an end. We're not going to just keep on fighting some global war against the evils of terrorism for the next fifty thousand years. God has a plan to win . . . and to win *completely*.

In the book *God: A Biography*, Steven Mosley writes: "When we hear of some child molester killing his third victim, or see newsfilm of bloated bodies sprawled on some southern Asian killing field, we get angry. Evil hurts. It makes us feel violated, outraged. But our indignation is only a shadow of the pain God feels. For the Being whose life is one righteous flame, every moral failing brings anguish. For the One obsessed with goodness, sin cuts deep" (p. 103).

And then Mosley concludes: "God IS a consuming fire. We are left naked and anxious with the ancient question, 'Who can stand in His presence?' "

This takes us to one of the most difficult truths in the Bible. Especially after what has happened to our world in 2001, people are talking about the doctrine of hellfire. As we consider the good temper of God, His righteous anger, we can be grateful that the Bible assures us God has a plan to end evil. Hellfire is going to be used by God to cleanse this world of sin, to sweep away the mountain of iniquity that's built up for six thousand years. The rubble of our rebellion will be swept away. And from that point of view, Christians who stand under the safe shadow of the Cross can be glad for this doctrine. Thank God He has a plan! Thank God He has the moral anger and the moral strength to bring this war to a close! The last thing we would ever want would be to limp along for the next millennium, from the year 2000 to the year 3000, while sin continues to taunt us.

But does God indeed have it within His divine power to really and truly *end* sin? Can He finish it—or does an eternally burning hell keep sin going throughout all eternity?

Maybe this is an area in which you've done some careful study, and you are to be saluted if you have. I serve God's church in a small denomination, and am certainly not a trained theologian, but let me humbly share where I am coming from in my own Bible study. I do not believe—and this is the doctrinal position of my Seventh-day Adventist Church family—that the Word of the Lord teaches the doctrine of a literal hellfire that goes on and on and on for all time through the ages. And although I cannot resolve with you this huge debate point in a page or so, let me simply open my heart to you and share one of the main reasons for our Church's position.

The pages of Scripture, as I read *all* the verses that speak to this topic—are clear. God is *not helpless* to bring sin to a final end. The idea that hellfire would go on forever, with sinners in the flames forever, continuing to scream and curse God and continuing to sin forever—that concept undercuts the very nature and power of God. Our heavenly Father intends to *win* against sin, not live in stalemate with it throughout all eternity.

In verse after verse in the Bible, we read that God plans to exercise His divine power to completely eradicate all traces of sin from the universe. Revelation 20:9: "Fire came down from heaven and *devoured* them [sinners]" (NIV, emphasis supplied).

In Matthew 10:28 Jesus is talking: " 'Do not be afraid of those who kill the body but cannot kill the soul. Rather, be afraid of the One [God] who can *destroy* both soul and body in hell' " (NIV, emphasis supplied).

2 Peter 3:10: "The day of the Lord will come like a thief. The heavens will disappear with a roar; the elements will be *destroyed* by fire, and the earth and everything in it will be laid bare" (NIV, emphasis supplied).

2 Thessalonians 1:9: "[Sinners] will be punished with everlasting *destruction*" (NIV, emphasis supplied).

In fact, as I look through my Bible concordance, the word *destruction* is used over and over again. God is capable, the Bible says, of absolutely destroying sin, consuming it, obliterating it. Sin and sinners will be destroyed, we're told.

Nobody rejoices over this Bible teaching. It's a terrible thing for anyone to perish in the flames at the end; we don't want that. It would be wonderful if every citizen of this planet would choose Jesus Christ as their Savior and be saved. But we can't ignore the teachings of the Bible. " 'Wide is the gate and broad is the way that leads to destruction,' " Jesus says, " 'and there are many who go in by it' " (Matthew 7:13, NKJV). Still, we can be thankful that God does intend to move, to bring the stain of sin to an end. Would we really want for Osama bin Laden and his network of followers to exist anywhere in God's universe for the ceaseless ages? Wouldn't you prefer for these rebels to simply be *gone?*

Second, let me add very humbly: I know there are other views on this Bible topic. I fully understand that. Your church may teach this doctrine in a completely different way; you may have a different perspective, and I accept that and praise God that you, too, are studying. No denomination on earth is correct in all its teachings. It would be arrogant to think we're right on everything; we need the Holy Spirit to guide our minds at all times.

Despite possible differences of opinion about how God eradicates sin, our discussions can continue in a spirit of love, and we can agree on this point: How important it is to be on God's side! How vital to cling to the Cross! In the end, He will do what He chooses to do, and what He chooses will be fair and right and worthy of our approval and our worship. This doctrine need not cause us fear if we are trusting in the blood of Jesus Christ, the Lamb of God, for our salvation and our eternal security. What a wonderful thing to have the good temper of God always active in our defense!

5

We Don't Lose Wars!

Have you ever seen a football game where your team is on the 50-yard line trying to go down the field for a touchdown? First and ten. But on the first play, somebody's called for holding: a 10-yard penalty. Now it's first and twenty. You run another play, and the same player is flagged again for holding. OK, now it's first and thirty. The quarterback cranks things up again, and this time the ball carrier is caught behind the line for a loss. Now it's second down and thirty-three, and your team has "progressed," so to speak, from the 50 all the way back to their own 27-yard line.

One thing is for sure: if that trend continues, your team's not going to win.

Maybe your team is on the 50-yard line, and on first down you make one yard. On second down, the running back gets one more yard. Third down, you get maybe half a yard. Meanwhile, the clock is showing 52 seconds left, and you're still down by ten points.

We come to the same conclusion. Your football team is 52 seconds away from another losing game. You can't win scoring one yard at a time when you can't keep up with the clock.

Many people in the Christian faith feel exactly that way about what we call the Great Commission. In Matthew 24:14, Jesus told His disciples—

and us—what it was going to take to win the football game: " 'This gospel of the kingdom will be preached *in the whole world* as a testimony to *all nations,* and then the end will come' " (NIV, emphasis supplied).

Just four chapters later, Jesus issues the same challenge again, and this time He ups the ante quite a little bit. " 'Go and *make disciples* of all nations' " (Matthew 28:19, NIV).

So this is talking about the real thing. Actually going, physically going, to every nation, preaching the gospel in person, walking with people down the aisle to the altar, baptizing them, nurturing them, discipling them. There isn't a TV shortcut we can take. Even Christian radio and TV being on all around the globe and throughout the former Soviet Union and blanketing the vast territories of Africa and China with shortwave doesn't really fulfill this verse's challenge. Making disciples in all nations is what it takes to win the game.

And when you look at the game plan on paper, it just plain looks like we can't win. You'd have to conclude that the cause of Christ is going to fold up. Especially after the tragedy of September 11, when the world is so convulsed by religious hatred.

Question: Is your own local Christian church growing as fast as the population in your state or province? Are baptisms keeping up with funerals? Are people coming in the front door faster than they're going out the backdoor—or is it the other way around?

Of course, we're most interested in how it is in our own personal lives. We want to grow in Jesus Christ, to grow in grace. We want to become mature Christians who graduate from milk to solid food, as the apostle Paul admonishes in 1 Corinthians 3. So we have to ask ourselves: Is it happening? Is it happening as fast as we'd like? Are we heading toward the Super Bowl, in terms of personal spiritual success? Are our lives as victorious as we wish they were, or is our team going backward on the football field, in the spiritual battlefield, the theater of operations?

The good news is this: *We serve a God who can't be beaten!* Heaven's motto always is, and always has been, WE DON'T LOSE WARS! God cannot lose! He's not going to lose! Despite how it looks right now on planet Earth, there's abundant evidence that He's not going to be beaten—and that those who ally themselves with Him aren't going to lose either.

A little-known promise from the Old Testament is part of the evidence. "The Lord thy God in the midst of thee is mighty; he will save." Maybe you prefer the NIV rendition: " 'The Lord your God is with you, he is mighty to save' " (Zephaniah 3:17).

And we all rejoice in this promise, echoing through the centuries from the original triumphant shout by the apostle Paul: "If God be for us, who can be against us?" (Romans 8:31).

I sometimes get a picture in old sci-fi films on television of the unbeatable nature of the Lord's campaign. In the *Back to the Future* trilogy, a kid named Marty McFly, played by Michael J. Fox, travels into the past and the future via a DeLorean time machine. And you see this thread in which sometimes the future could be changed, the so-called space-time continuum . . . and sometimes it couldn't be changed. He'd try to prevent something terrible from happening—because he knows it's about to—and he runs out of gas.

But I actually find in this odd little story that same powerful Bible truth. *God is going to win.* That is a fixed truth. It can't be changed; it can't be overcome; it can't be undone. The fact of God's victory is concrete truth that you can hold on to today. Even as the world lurches tentatively into this new kind of war against an enemy that doesn't stand in neat rows on a battlefield, we can know that God doesn't lose wars.

There are battles in the war between Christ and His enemy—Satan—that are still in the future. They haven't happened yet. And one might think that those future events are subject to alteration. A great heroic effort, or a demonic one, could overturn them—you would think. And then you couple that fear with the ongoing reality that the church of Christ is struggling here in the very beginnings of the twenty-first century. The devil is winning battles all over the place. Things are shaky for the people of God.

And yet the Bible promises about ultimate victory are absolute, unshakeable, unchangeable truth.

In the book of Revelation, especially starting in chapter 19, we find ringing promises that tell us God simply *is not* going to lose. Chapter 19 describes the Rider on the white horse, Jesus Christ. And He's followed by the armies of heaven. They don't come down here to lose; they come down here to *win.*

Chapter 20, verses 8-10, describes the final battle: Armageddon. What happens? God wins, the devil loses.

Chapters 21 and 22 contain more descriptions of the victory, not only for God, but for God's people. Those who are allied with God will share in His victory: " 'Now the dwelling of God is with men, and he will live with them. They will be his people, and God himself will be with them and be their God. He will wipe every tear from their eyes. There will be no more death or mourning or crying or pain, for the old order of things has passed away' " (Revelation 21:3, 4, NIV).

I hope this doesn't sound flip or casual, but I almost see God's enemy in terms of that kid driving around helplessly in the time-traveling DeLorean. No matter where he is in the space-time continuum, no matter what he tries to do, the devil just keeps losing. He's the Flat-Tire King of all time. Every strategy he tries backfires! In fact, even when he wins . . . he loses.

Let's go to the Garden of Eden. We see the devil's DeLorean parked outside the front gate behind a bush. And he wins a little battle; Adam and Eve sin and become his captives. Then what? In the very same chapter, a Redeemer is promised. Jesus will win them back. And the serpent's victory turns into defeat.

Travel down through time a couple of thousand years. There's that same DeLorean parked on a sand dune by the Red Sea. The children of Israel are trapped: mountains all around, the sea in front of them, the Egyptian army behind them and closing in quickly. The devil can't lose this time! Except that God opens up the Red Sea, then closes it just in time to swallow up the whole enemy army. Another blockbuster loss.

Now we move to Jesus in that Garden of Gethsemane, and then on the cross of Calvary. This looks like the biggest enemy win of all history. Jesus is dead in the tomb; the war's over. Satan has won! But it turns out not to be. The resurrected Son of God comes *out* of the tomb. Darkness turns into light. Tragedy becomes triumph. And all Satan can do is watch in bitter frustration from the sidelines as his biggest campaign fails. No matter what he tries, *God simply will not be beaten.*

In the early Christian church, God's followers are persecuted and tortured and killed. The battlefield is covered with blood. But for every Christian soldier who falls, a hundred new ones spring up to take his or her place. The blood of those martyrs waters the meadows of the Dark Ages, and the church actually grows and thrives. Satan simply can't win.

It's the year 1517. The medieval church is locked in heresy and superstition; the enemy has managed to infiltrate it with pagan practices and false teachings. He's on the verge of a huge triumph. But then October 31 comes around, and a monk named Martin Luther nails ninety-five theses to the church door in Wittenburg. The Protestant Reformation is born; the pure Christian church is revived. Satan was so close—and he loses again.

And now the same scenario is being played out again. Maybe it's happening in your life. Lucifer is attacking you; he's pelting you with temptations and discouragement. Maybe he's hitting you with the temptation to seek a divorce or with a habit you just can't break. Maybe you lost a loved one in the attack on the World Trade Center, and your heart is breaking as you finally fill out the paperwork so that your spouse can be declared dead, and you can receive the survivor's benefits. All hope is finally gone, and with your heart breaking, you go to the community bulletin boards and take down the photos of the man you loved so much. And at this very moment, Satan is so close to victory, because you're about ready to give up.

But our enemy pushes you just a little bit too far. His hatred overshadows his wisdom and his craftiness. He's so close to enslaving you for good, but that last temptation, that last trial is just one too many. And you're so discouraged, so in despair that the devil actually drives you down onto your knees. That's right! He pushes you to your knees—and you cry out, "Jesus, save me!"

I've seen this time after time; in fact, I've experienced it in my own life! The devil doesn't know when to quit, and he sabotages his own campaigns! He ends up losing in the very projects he starts. He steps on his own land mines.

I want to tell you *half* of my favorite expression. Just half. And here it is: "Satan is mighty."

Would you agree with that? He *is* mighty! He *is* a mighty foe! The book of 1 Peter describes Satan as an enemy, an adversary, a roaring lion capable of devouring us. He's a dangerous enemy; he's not to be trifled with. Lucifer is a very real being, a tangible enemy, a formidable foe. He's the prince of darkness. Yes, *Satan is mighty*. But praise God, because that's only half of my favorite saying. And you know what the entire saying is. *Satan is mighty, but Jesus is ALMIGHTY!*

Wherever you are today, know this to be true. Satan is mighty. He absolutely is. But Jesus Christ is ALMIGHTY. And when it comes to war, *almighty* beats *mighty* every single time.

Have you ever played that old, kid's card game, ironically called "War"? You pull out a card, and then your opponent pulls one out—and the higher card wins. And every time Satan pulls out a six, God has a seven. Satan gets a king, and God has an ace. Every time! He doesn't lose!

In *The Knowledge of the Holy,* A. W. Tozer points out that the King James Version of the Bible uses the word *almighty* fifty-six times. And all fifty-six are in reference to God (p. 165). Not to us; not to a great king like David or Solomon. Not to the twelve disciples. Not to George W. Bush or Osama bin Laden. And not even to the devil. The devil is mighty, but God is almighty. He doesn't ever lose. No matter where you park your DeLorean and get out, you see God winning again.

Maybe we could express the power of God in terms of "odds." I have a fond childhood memory of playing Monopoly® with my dad and three brothers. In the 1960s we were missionaries in Bangkok, and the whole family was quarantined with the mumps. We had nothing to do but sit in the living room in our pajamas and play endless rounds of the Parker Brothers classic.

And in that particular Monopoly marathon, we began to notice what a good property the orange cards are: St. James, Tennessee, and New York. And the reason is obvious. If you're in Jail, or even just visiting, those three orange properties are right down the street within throwing distance. If you roll a six, or an eight, or a nine, you're going to be paying the owner of the Oranges. With a hotel, it can set you back 950 bucks, or a cool one grand on New York Avenue.

But something very interesting happens so often—which I'm sure you've noticed if you've ever owned those Oranges. So often a person coming out of Jail will roll a seven—and land right in between the Oranges on Community Chest. Not a six, not an eight, not a nine . . . he rolls a seven. And you don't collect a single dime.

It took me years of frustration before I realized that when you have two dice, which means thirty-six possible number combinations, rolling a seven is the most common number on there. (Any frequent visitor to Las Vegas can tell you that, but I was an innocent missionary kid.) Six out of the thirty-six combinations are a seven. Maybe you never thought about that either, but if you own those Orange properties and are hoping someone comes to stay in your $950 hotel, you begin to notice it in a hurry. The odds are pretty good for rolling a seven. Now, 39 percent of the time, you will roll a six, eight, or nine, but seven is still the most common number.

It is human nature to be very interested in stories in which someone wins against all the odds. Some of the great war sagas happen when a tiny army of one thousand goes up against ten thousand—and wins! A person with a handicap works and struggles and battles against the odds—and ends up winning an Olympic gold medal. A Helen Keller, blind, deaf, and mute, beats the unbelievable odds stacked up against her—and becomes an articulate and effective communicator.

And yes, the Christian faith is facing some very long odds today. An exploding world population is dwarfing our minuscule achievements. Every day and every year, it seems, the Body of Christ is falling further and further behind. Vast regions of the world simply will not allow missionaries in—and where they do let them in, society is rigidly entrenched against the message they bring. In the weeks following the terrorist attacks, a devastating "sidebar" followed the story of two young Christian aid workers in Afghanistan, behind bars for the simple "crime" of allegedly trying to share the gospel message.

So God's people face a stacked deck. On the global battlefield, the devil's odds can be a frightful thing. But here is a powerful postscript to the news that God does not lose wars. Guess what? *God doesn't care about odds!*

To God the concept of heavy-odds-against-you doesn't matter. A thousand to one—doesn't matter! A million to one—doesn't matter! Odds simply are not a factor to God. And we find some great, down-to-earth Bible stories about this very simple truth.

Consider the Old Testament story of Gideon, found in Judges 6 and 7. The Bible doesn't tell us how big an army the Midianites had. But Gideon had 32,000 men—and he was nervous. So already they must have been facing bad odds.

But then God says: "Send some of these men home."

"What!"

"You heard Me. Send some of them home." All the scared GIs, 22,000 of them, pick up their canteens and their M-16s and they head back home to their families and girlfriends. So now Gideon has only 10,000 men. And the odds go from bad to terrible.

God says: "You've still got too many men, Gideon."

"Oh, no! Lord, You're kidding."

"Too many men. Send some more home." And the dust doesn't settle for quite a while, as nine thousand seven hundred more men pack up their pup tents and their infrared night goggles and their Sidewinder missiles, and they leave too. Now Gideon is down to 300 men. Three hundred versus however many tens of thousands the Midianites have recruited. Now these aren't terrible odds, they're astronomical odds. There's no way to win.

Except for the fact that God doesn't care about odds. Three hundred against a million is no problem as long as God is with the 300. And now when Israel wins, which they do, God gets the credit—which was the whole point of the story.

Flip through a few more pages to 1 Kings 18. Elijah is on top of Mount Carmel, facing down 450 false prophets of Baal and 400 more prophets of the pagan god Asherah. That's 850-to-one odds right there. Plus the king and queen of Israel, Ahab and a certain power-hungry woman named Jezebel, are in the opposition camp. That makes it 852 to one. Those are pretty bad odds. But even when you add twelve big jars of water to the mix, the fire from the Lord still consumes Elijah's offering. He still triumphs! With God on his side, odds of 852 to one are absolutely no problem.

This is why we can look at the exploding world population and the oppression experienced by Christians in certain countries and the secularization of our own society here at home and the destroyed portion of the Pentagon and determine in our hearts not to worry! The Christian church faces heavy odds, but odds are not a problem with God. He has promised that the gospel will be taken to the entire world; He's promised in Matthew 24 to cut the time short for the sake of His people; He's promised to come again.

But of course, you and I are even more concerned about the odds in our own lives. Maybe you have a problem with anger. And it's hereditary; you've always struggled with it. Thoughts of rage and resentment seem to simply seize your mind; they won't leave you alone. Every aspect of your life, your job, your marriage, your family feeds that frustration, that boiling over. And you want to cry to the heavens: "This is a hopeless problem! God, even You couldn't fix what I struggle with. This is insurmountable;

it's a million-to-one long shot."

But God doesn't care about odds! Whether it's alcoholism or jealousy or smoking or some other quiet, agonizing addiction—God can beat the odds on your behalf.

That doesn't mean victory will be quick. It might be—and it might not be. There have been trusting believers who reached out and took God's hand, and a forty-year smoking habit was snuffed out just like that. Other people have had to battle cravings for years—but they kept holding God's hand. And with God, victory isn't just possible—it's promised. It's assured.

When you're in that Monopoly game and your little token is on the "Just Visiting" Jail square, and you look down at those terrifying Orange properties, enemy properties, with their hotels—it's a scary thing. My dad was both a devout Christian preacher and a born-again "shark" with the little white cubes. "Educated dice," he would say with a grin . . . and confidently roll that seven. Or a ten and collect all the accumulated cash in Free Parking. But most of us stare into a future of Orange Hotels, severe temptations, major bills, and bankruptcy. Maybe we'll beat the odds, and maybe we won't. Our confidence has evaporated; this is a nerve-racking moment.

Isn't it wonderful that with God, we never have to feel that way again?

And how does that feel when we get so close to the end? God has won; that means His people have won too. We're in a great army, under a General who can't be beaten. There's still some mopping up to be done, still some skirmishes to fight. In fact, there's actually a very major battle yet in the future. But in the war itself, a Victor has already been declared.

Here in Los Angeles, when the L.A. Lakers play a basketball game, sometimes you come down to the last few minutes, and the home team finally has a lead that isn't going to get away. Announcer Chick Hearn has always had his trademark way of announcing that, in his opinion, the Lakers have just reached that point. "The game is in the refrigerator," he announces to his listeners. "The door's closed, the light is out, the eggs are cooling, the Jell-O's jiggling, and the butter's getting hard." And fans watching on television give out a cry of triumph. "Yes! This ballgame's ours! We've won."

It's good news that when God wins, His people win too. His victory is our victory; His assurance is something we can claim in our own lives.

When you watch NBA games on television, notice how the fans sitting in the bleachers are reacting. They're not playing the game; they're not getting a salary from the Lakers. They don't wear championship rings. But you try telling the fans that this isn't *their* victory! In fact, in many stadiums, when the last out is made or the clock runs out, immediately the huge Diamond Vision scoreboard reads, "WE win!" In other words, all of us. The victory belongs to the fans as well.

What does it mean to us as Christian soldiers, knowing that God is going to win? If you're marching under His banner, then this is the time to have confidence! Don't give up! Stand tall! You're marching with the winners.

There are some wonderful missionary stories of Christians who ended up in internment camps during World War II. *Behind Barbed Wire,* about John and Barbara Oss, is one of my favorites. And when those captives of many different faith groups saw the first Allied planes fly over their camp and dip their wings as if to say, "Hang on!" a great shout of victory went through the entire camp. And all the guards and the prison commandant just stood by helplessly. They knew it was over too.

Right now, take the reality that *God doesn't lose wars* and just clutch it to your heart. Make it your own! Let that good news fill your life and become part of your own outlook, your own spiritual confidence.

In Isaiah 49 we read this wartime statement coming from our own God: "But this is what the Lord says: 'Yes, captives will be taken from warriors, and plunder retrieved from the fierce; I will contend with those who contend with you, and your children I will save' " (verse 25, NIV).

"Do you have enemies?" God asks. Enemies in the form of temptations, habits, spiritual challenges? Are the bullets flying dangerously close to your head? Do terrorists seem to have you in their sights? Our warrior God promises us, "Friend, your enemies will become My enemies. I will contend with those who contend with you. I will fight for you."

God fighting for me and fighting for you—that's quite a promise, isn't it? Especially when you remember that God doesn't ever lose wars.

6

Where Were You Tuesday Morning, God?

It has become an anthem for some following the terrorist attacks on America: "Imagine" by John Lennon. It was sung by Neil Young in the all-networks benefit concert ten days later, and bitter people around the world are keying in on the one verse that "imagines" no countries, nothing to kill or die for, and no religion.

Atheists are tired of having "God Bless America" sung at all sporting events; they resent President Bush telling a watching world that "God is not neutral."

According to Ellen Johnson, president of American Atheists, which is "the country's oldest organization for nonbelievers," says an *L.A. Times* story by Hector Becerra, "If [the attack] wasn't a wake-up call to a religious nation, I don't know what is. That said to me, 'There is no God.' Where was He, on a coffee break? She and others are putting up on their banners the statement by Robert Ingersoll: 'Hands that help are better far than lips that pray.' "

In the same article, Becerra quotes a self-proclaimed atheist named Randi Mendelsohn, who lives in nearby Staten Island and was personally affected by the collapse of the World Trade Center. "Getting home and hearing the President recite the 23rd Psalm angered her. 'During the national day of prayer, what was I supposed to do?' she asked. 'Is praying the answer? To what? Has it helped yet? Are we better now?' "

Those are painfully relevant questions. And Christians are too prone to give the same pat answers over and over.

Morris Venden tells a story that is painfully personal. His daughter Lynn has a congenital handicap that couldn't be treated medically, and so it was a source of great difficulty and spiritual trial to the entire family.

And for years, by Pastor Venden's own confession, he shrank away from really offering up a specific prayer of intercession for her to be healed. Yes, he knew all about the Bible texts and promises regarding healing; after all, he'd preached them for years. But this was his own flesh and blood, his own daughter. He wondered if he had enough faith. Were his motives pure enough? What if the family prayed and God said "No"? Could they take not only the disappointment, but also the spiritual faith crisis that might follow?

For several years, his daughter kept begging him to have that kind of prayer service for her. "I'm old enough to understand," she told him. "I know it might not be God's will to heal me, and that's OK. I'm ready to pray, 'Jesus, Thy will be done.' Why can't we do it?"

Finally the family gathered up their courage. Several of the church elders and close family friends came over, and they read their Bibles together and confessed their sins. Then they all prayed for Lynn to be healed if it was God's will.

It became clear almost immediately that God, in His own wisdom, had decided to say "No" to their request. His daughter was not healed, and true to her word, she accepted that without complaint or any bitterness. Even now she is bravely carrying on, knowing that Christ will heal her at the Second Coming.

But as Venden relates the anecdote in his book *The Answer Is Prayer,* just as that group of Christians finished their prayer for his daughter's healing, something wonderful happened. It had been a rainy, overcast day. But as they said Amen and waited to sense God's reply, the sunlight broke through the window and bathed his daughter in what seemed to be Heaven's presence. It was as though God had said, "My child, I heard your request. Please trust Me that My 'No' is the right answer for you; but I *did* hear you, and I love you" (pp. 126, 127).

That's a beautiful story, but we wrestle with the stories that aren't so beautiful. Christians accept that God sometimes says "No." And any time we pray, saying—as we're taught to—"Thy will be done," Heaven might indeed choose to say "No" to our human requests. Some people barely missed getting on Flight 11, and praise God for His "providence." But what about the eighty-one passengers who did get to Logan Airport and get on board a plane with five hijackers?

When God says "No," it is difficult enough. But what do we do when God seems to say *nothing?* Not "No," but *nothing?* We pray, and there's no evidence that Heaven even heard. We're not sure if that prayer request even got out of our own driveway, let alone to heaven's pearly gates Fifty trillion miles away. We hear nothing; we feel nothing; we sense nothing.

The Bible tells stories of people, even great spiritual champions, who prayed and then felt that way. King David was sometimes almost desperate to know that God hears and is answering. In Psalm 22:1 we glimpse how even this man after God's own heart felt that the door to heaven was locked up tight and sealed up against him. And he cries out with words of bewilderment, "My God, my God, why have you forsaken me?" (NIV). Does that sound familiar? Even Jesus Himself quoted those words on the cross as He, too, cried out to an unresponsive Heaven. David continues: "Why are you so far from saving me, so far from the words of my groaning? O my God, I cry out by day, but you do not answer, by night, and am not silent" (verses 1, 2, NIV).

No, the psalmist isnot silent, but Heaven is. There's no answer. No message on the phone machine: "We're not in right now, but your call is very important. Leave your name and number, etc." No celestial voicemail service promises prompt attention and assures us that our business is important to Heaven. Nothing like that. Just an awful silence ringing in our ears.

And here's another disturbing thought. There are some Christians who, if you ask them, can never really point to a single tangible answer to prayer for them. They can't even be sure that God is saying "No"; for all the evidence shows, there may just not be anyone at all on the other end of the prayer line. They're hitting the SEND button to fire off emails to heaven, but they've never gotten a single answer back in their own mailbox. Nothing but silence. Is God's computer even on? How long should they continue in the Christian faith if there's no proof that Somebody is out there?

In his book *When God Says No,* Pastor Leith Anderson tells some wonderful stories of answered prayer. Sometimes it seems so easy! An opening anecdote goes like this:

A Muslim convert to Christianity received a phone call in 1990 that his neighborhood was on fire and his house soon would burn. He rushed from his government office to see the flames closing in. There was time to save only his most precious belongings, and when he ran into his house he salvaged a mattress. Standing outside, surrounded by the Muslim neighbors who had persecuted him, he lifted his hands and voice and prayed out loud in the name of Jesus Christ, asking God to intervene and save his home. When he finished with "in Jesus' name. Amen" the thunder boomed, the rains poured and the flames were extinguished.

And Pastor Anderson adds, in what's got to be a delightful understatement: "The neighbors were impressed."

Well, that's very nice, but it doesn't go that way all the time. There are fifty million "flip sides" to that kind of miracle story. And this same writer concedes as much. Perhaps something in this next list resonates with you:

> Those who are so gravely disappointed with God usually aren't evil people. They are mothers and fathers who sincerely believe God could and would heal their children from terminal diseases. They are missionaries praying for success in evangelizing the peoples to whom God has called them. They are children who kneel beside their beds at night and ask God to give Daddy a new job or to stop him from hurting Mommy. They are police officers who pray for protection, students who ask for help in their exams, relief workers who plead for food to feed starving families and government leaders who seek divine wisdom in controversial legislative votes. They are good, well-intentioned people, and we would be hard pressed to label their prayers as anything but good and reasonable. We see no clear-cut reasons why God would turn them down.

But often God does turn them down. You and I could paste many heartbreaking post-September 11 stories into that paragraph as well—stories of people who prayed for the safety and well-being of their loved ones, only to realize with horror that one of the four downed planes had scarred their futures forever.

And how does God say His "No's"? Two lessons loom large.

First of all, even if the sun doesn't break through the clouds, we know the sun is still there behind those clouds. It was wonderful that Heaven gave the Venden family assurance of God's love and presence, but the presence would have been just as real without that moment of rare sunshine. And it takes a special Christian to accept that the Son—now spelled S - O - N—is present even if clouds are there today and even if clouds linger for the next month or year or decade. A loving God is always there, no matter what we may hear or see or feel.

Second, let's learn from a young girl's willingness to pray with those four words: "Thy will be done." In fact, Pastor Leith Anderson teaches his church flock this explicit prayer: "Lord, today I choose to will *Your* will."

Of course, it is so much easier to advise other Christians to pray that prayer than it is to pray it yourself through the dark midnight of your own loss.

Shadowlands is one of the most wrenching roller-coaster rides of emotion ever recorded in book or film. The Christian writer C. S. Lewis, after a very brief, cancer-threatened marriage to his beloved Joy Gresham, knelt at her bedside as she passed away on a horrible Wednesday, July 13, 1960. The love of his life was gone. By his own admission, he was like a sleepwalker, numb with grief and loneliness.

He was a man who had served God and written passionately and eloquently about the Christian faith for all of his adult life. Millions of readers had come to know God better through the pen of Jack Lewis. And this brilliant scholar had felt the hand of God, personal and loving, on his own shoulder, guiding him out of atheism and into the light of Christianity.

And all at once, after the funeral of Joy—nothing. God was gone. Absolutely and terrifyingly gone. He prayed and felt nothing. Heard nothing. Sensed nothing. And it was a fierce, hostile nothing, one that threatened to undo everything he'd ever believed.

Maybe you saw the Richard Attenborough film where Lewis, portrayed by Anthony Hopkins, comes into a room, and his colleagues—all of the dear, grieving friends—are waiting for him. And one of them makes a comforting remark about God's love. All at once C. S. Lewis almost pounces on him. "No!" It's a terrible shriek. "It won't do! It's a bloody mess and that's all there is to it."

Later he writes down his feelings in a book entitled *A Grief Observed*. His spiritual musings from twenty years earlier, from the safety of comfortable bachelorhood, now are painfully real. "Where is God when it hurts?" he had wondered before. Now he really wonders.

And when he prayed—nothing. God wasn't saying "No" to him, as He had seemed to do when Jack begged Him to heal Joy. Now God wasn't saying anything. It felt, Lewis wrote, like a door being slammed in his face. In fact, he could almost hear heaven bolting and double-bolting the door against him. The keys to the kingdom clicking in twenty locks to make sure not a word from C. S. Lewis might get through. "Go away, Jack" was posted on every corner of the kingdom. His brother Warnie had retreated to alcohol; his two stepsons, Douglas and David, were immersed in their own grief; his friends were staying away. And now even God was mysteriously, almost cruelly, gone (pp. 4, 5).

What do we do with this silent God? People in my little Ojai Valley Adventist Church need healing, they need comfort, they need financial blessings, they long for wayward children to come back to Jesus. And many of them have felt the silence of God. Which is perhaps why they turn to the rest of us during "sharing time" as friends. "Here!" they cry out, handing their heart's greatest ache over to the congregation. "I'm just one person. My voice is too feeble and frail, I guess. God doesn't hear me, but maybe He'll hear you."

All we have are human insights. Which, of course, is our problem. We're human beings looking at our messed-up world through human eyes. We don't know where Heaven is coming from; we don't see the entire pattern, the divine mosaic. We see the hollow craters of September 11 through our own narrow telescope. And so God's ways make no sense to us. His silence baffles us and hurts us. In Philip Yancey's book *Disappointment With God,* he poses exactly three blunt, unvarnished questions: "Is God unfair? Is God hidden? Is God silent?" (p. 30).

A dedicated Christian, and even a biblical giant like the apostle Paul, couldn't help but notice that the "No's" of prayer often seem to come to God's most faithful servants. Paul himself prayed in 2 Corinthians 12 that God would take away a very personal and painful problem: "To keep me from becoming conceited because of these surpassingly great revelations, there was given me a thorn in my flesh, a messenger of Satan, to torment me. Three times I pleaded with the Lord to take it away from me. But he said to me, 'My grace is sufficient for you, for my power is made perfect in weakness' " (Verses 7-9, NIV).

It might well have been the third prayer before God cleared His throat to tell Paul No. Paul himself might have experienced the silence of God when he asked Him earlier. But now God finally tells him: "It's 'No,' and it's always going to be 'No.' "

One of the most courageous of Bible heroes, a man named Job, got silence from God. A great debate, a chess game for the ages, was going on between God and Lucifer—and Job didn't know he was the pawn. But one of the great examples of solid faith, a champion mentioned in the "Who's Who" faith lineup of Hebrews 11, got silence from heaven. In Job 19:7, 8, halfway through this horrible ordeal, he confessed to his so-called friends: " 'Though I cry, "I've been wronged!" I get no response; though I call for help, there is no justice. He has blocked my way so I cannot pass; he has shrouded my paths in darkness' " (NIV).

And we ask, Why does God treat one of His best friends this way? Why shouldn't the faithful followers get God's private number, the secret code word, the email address no one else knows? Countries around the world seek Most Favored Nation status with the United Sstates; shouldn't Christians get similar preferential treatment from Heaven?

In his book *The Efficacy of Prayer,* C. S. Lewis explores this very question. What would it look like to the world if Christians did get favored status from God, got their prayers answered with more "Yes's" than their heathen neighbors? "It would be even worse to think of those who get what they pray for as a sort of court favorites, people who have influence with the throne. The refused prayer of Christ in Gethsemane is answer enough for that." Then he adds: "And I dare not leave out the hard saying which I once heard from an experienced Christian." The friend had said this: "I have seen many striking answers to prayer and more than one that I thought miraculous. But they usually come at the beginning: before conversion, or soon after it. As the Christian life proceeds, they tend to be rarer. The refusals, too, are not only more frequent; they become more unmistakable, more emphatic."

Lewis himself had felt that emphatic silence, the hard quiet of God's "No" to him in his darkest hour. He writes:

> Does God then forsake just those who serve Him best? Well, He who served Him best of all said, near His tortured death, "Why hast thou forsaken Me?" When God becomes man, that Man, of all others,

is least comforted by God, at His greatest need. There is a mystery here which, even if I had the power, I might not have the courage to explore. Meanwhile, little people like you and me, if our prayers are sometimes granted, beyond all hope and probability, had better not draw hasty conclusions to our own advantage. If we were stronger, we might be less tenderly treated. If we were braver, we might be sent, with far less help, to defend far more desperate posts in the great battle (quoted from "The Business of Heaven: Daily Readings," p. 481, contained in *The Inspirational Writings of* C. S. Lewis).

This is heavy business, but sometimes God's best soldiers do get the hardest assignments. Others who are weak, spiritual infants, or even still in the rebel camp, might get kid-glove treatment, get almost *babied* by the Almighty. But a man like Job, a mighty warrior of faith, got that hardest battle, that most distant and barren of outposts, where there wasn't mail or phones or anything. And God, looking down at the arrows and enemy torment, I'm sure whispered—though Job couldn't hear Him—"Hold on, Job. You're My man. Hold on. When the time is right—*My* time—I'll rescue you. You'll hear from Me then; I promise. Until then, hold on."

There was a gritty, hard-to-read story in the the December 1997 *Reader's Digest* (pp.143–148). A young mother named Barbara received two diagnoses virtually at once. Her physician said she had a very serious case of leukemia. And her midwife told her that she was pregnant—with twins.

Barb's dilemma was this: If she got on a bone-marrow transplant program immediately for the leukemia, it would require aborting the two little babies already growing inside of her. There was simply no time to lose.

Well, after much prayer and discussion and searching of souls, she and her husband, Jeff, decided to keep both babies and to postpone the medical treatment until after the births, which were still quite a few months away. In the meantime, they could fight that killer white-blood-cell count of 200,000 with a centrifuge procedure called leukapheresis and also oral chemotherapy, but the bone-marrow transplant operation was put off for the sake of those two fetuses. This was a wrenching and very personal choice, and certainly you and I wouldn't have argued much with a couple that made another decision.

Certainly many, many prayers went up during those seven months of waiting . . . and waiting . . . and waiting. Knowing all the time that the leukemia was still lurking in her system, that her chances of survival were growing dimmer by the week. And sure enough, six months after the twins Hunter and McKenzie were born, Barbara passed away on January 22, 1995. The father was left with a four-year-old son, Taylor, and those two little babies.

We sit in insulated comfort reading the article, and we toss down the *Reader's Digest* in frustration. Where is God? Why didn't He work a miracle? This is the thanks a family gets for valuing life, for sacrificing self? Why doesn't the silent God show Himself? If not now, when? If not for Barbara Barton, then for who?

There are many, many wonderful books out there that chronicle answers to prayer. And yes, we thank God for those stories. But there aren't many books with stories such as Barbara's, in which good, deserving people, lifetime Christians, have a legitimate prayer need, life-and-death—and heaven gives them absolutely no response. They encounter the silent God. God doesn't even seem to say "No"; He just plain doesn't answer at all. And the silence there in the emergency room or the morgue is nearly deafening.

One thing that makes this issue of God's silence even more difficult is the stark contrast we see with the miracle-packed pages of Scripture. It doesn't seem to be this way in the Bible! Not at all! People were healed right and left! Terrorists are turned back at every turn, nabbed at the airport X-ray machine, headed off at the pass.

Just one verse from the book of Matthew describes the sweeping nature of Jesus' healing ministry. "When evening came, many who were demon-possessed were brought to him [Jesus], and he drove out the spirits with a word and healed *all* the sick" (Matthew 8:16, NIV).

Every sick person who came to Him was made well. Jesus offered a 100 percent cure rate. There are passages suggesting that when Jesus went through this or that town, there wasn't a single sick person left when He left town. The hospitals were empty; the funeral parlors went out of business, and every crutch was turned into kindling wood. And if you go back just two verses in Matthew 8, the context to this healing marathon is that Jesus came into His disciple Peter's house and found that Peter's mother-in-law was in bed sick.

There was none of this "silent God." None of this "no answer"; "nobody home"; "one chance in twenty thousand of getting your prayer answered." No! "Jesus touched her hand and the fever left her" (verse 15) the Bible says. Of course! This was Peter's wife's mom! A friend! Of course

Jesus would heal her; why would there even be any discussion about it?

Again, sometimes today God does indeed allow His best soldiers to suffer on the hardest battlefields, without much apparent help from heaven's artilleries. The best Christians get the fewest answers, and we see God off in some other arena working miracles for the thieves and the hustlers and the madmen. And it's hard to realize that Heaven is trying to win those people and trusting that God's best soldiers will trust in Him even during difficult and lonely battles.

But a second, beautiful principle about God's silence is illustrated in a surprising place—in a Christian book on marriage: *Reclaiming Intimacy in Your Marriage,* by a husband-and-wife pastoral team, Robert and Debra Bruce. I use that word *team* on purpose, because it's a concept they often mention in this book. "We're the 'Bruce team.' " The talents or abilities missing in one of them, the other partner often has. When one struggled emotionally, the other one could pick him or her up. When they went through a hard time, they would remember how God had blessed them as a team in the past, and that gave them courage to keep on going.

In a chapter "Face Life's Interruptions . . . Together," they write about tragedies: deaths, financial downturns, lingering sicknesses, pain. And how some people get mad and blow up, while others face sorrow and pain in stoic silence.

But then they observe:

> There is a third and better way. Notice that we call this a "way" and not an "explanation." Arguments and explanations fall silent when we are in darkness, when life's interruptions hit, but we have experienced that there is always a light, a way, if you will. When we join hands together in an intimate marriage and look at this light, we realize that *we are not alone* (p. 228).

Then they add this wonderful spiritual principle:

> This light is what we call the "communion of saints." We know that in the midst of tragedy or crisis, we are surrounded by men and women, a "cloud of witnesses," who went through suffering, trusting boldly in God. They aren't here to offer us explanations,

69

but they have given us the testimony of their lives to point us to a Savior who can see us through to victory (p. 227).

That "cloud of witnesses" soundbite comes right from Hebrews 12, where the author reminds us that we are indeed on a tough course. It's a race, a difficult, arduous track, with rain and mud and tears and splinters. "We are surrounded by such a great cloud of witnesses," we're told in verse 1. "Let us run with perseverance the race marked out for us" (NIV).

That is a powerful bit of truth! Maybe you pray and God seems silent. You feel like you're getting no answer, that Heaven is saying "No" in a very cold and impersonal way. But the bottom-line truth is that God has answered many, many prayers! All through the ages He has answered prayers. Did He heal your relative? Maybe not—but God is a healing God. He *has* healed millions. In a world racked with sin, no, He doesn't heal everyone. Not yet anyway. But He has a healing heart, a loving heart. We are surrounded by a cloud of witnesses who call out to us: "He healed my daughter," "He healed my dad," "He healed *me!*"

Other witnesses tell how God rescued, how He intervened, how He sent angels, how He even brought loved ones back to life. If you're a Christian, part of the Body of Christ—this 2,000-year-old living, dynamic organism that spans the globe and the past twenty centuries—then you are surrounded by uncountable cases, millions of them, where God answered prayers of people who are part of your team! He said "Yes" as often as He dared, as often as His loving, all-knowing, divine plan would permit.

Of course, biblical concepts like "cloud of witnesses" offer spiritual answers but not necessarily practical help. "Cheap comfort," we say to the person offering the platitude. John Creamer, a high-school teacher in Worcester, Massachusetts, lost his pretty wife, Tara, in the World Trade Center attack. She made the bulk of the family's income as a successful planning manager at TJX. Now he has to raise Colin, age four, and baby Nora, fifteen months old, by himself. Child care expenses run $1,000 a month. An immigrant from Puerto Rico, Juan Nieves, age fifty-six, had built a good life in America, supporting his wife and four kids by making salads at the Windows on the World restaurant in the WTC. Now the family has $7,600 in savings and a 1968 Mustang the family will have to sell. And *Newsweek* magazine's article closes with the not-meant-to-be-trite phrase, "A nation wishes them godspeed" (October 8, 2001, p. 53).

But in grappling with our own downed phone lines to heaven, our own encounters with the silence of God, there are a couple points to ponder.

First, even to the grieving widow or to the parents who have lost an infant, God is not as silent as we may think. He is still an Answer-er of prayers, even though He didn't say "Yes" to this one particular prayer which admittedly meant so very much to us.

But we also ask for forgiveness of sins—which God always answers with a "Yes." We pray for God's Holy Spirit to fill us, and He says "Yes" again. We invite Him to have His way in our lives; He says "Yes." Our daily bread is still provided. We pray asking God to give us strength to obey His leading, and He responds positively.

Second, what must it mean to Heaven when heroes keep on trusting? With what dynamic power, are the false accusations of Satan shattered when men and women keep on trusting God through the silence and the fog? For long millennia now, Satan has screamed at the entire watching universe: "These earth people don't love God, don't trust Him! He's just a Santa Claus to them, a rigged slot machine. When the candy doesn't come out, they reject Him every time!"

But God can point to a man like Job, to a married couple who keep trusting God through that most painful of funerals. "Look at these trophies," He says quietly. "I *was* quiet with them; for a long time they didn't hear My voice. I said 'No' to their request, even though they actually deserved much better. But still they trust Me, they seek Me, they love Me. They've been in the shadows, in the fog, for a long, long time—but their faith hasn't wavered."

In some cosmic way, our faith during the silence is valuable to God beyond what we can imagine. God knows the value of such a soldier.

And Philip Yancey adds to this the keen truth that God doesn't exempt Himself from the same kinds of pain. Whatever we have experienced, He has too—through the Cross. In Jesus' sacrifice He has felt our pain a hundredfold (*Disappointment With God*, p. 217).

Wouldn't it be something to have that kind of faith, to be the kind of man or woman God could use to that level? Maybe we all shrink away from it; on the other hand, who knows which of us might be called to be a battlefield hero? Rabbi Abraham Heschel, looking on with great admiration at the experience of Job, said with deep reverence: "Faith like Job's cannot be shaken because it is the result of having *been* shaken" (ibid., pp. 247, 248). Isn't that tremendous?

In the end, there's one more truth to cling to. It is true that some of these books about our silent God don't really resolve all of our hurts, our frustration that the phone lines are down. You can read a masterpiece like *The Problem With Pain* and then go back and reread it and underline it, and still not be clear on why God so often seems absent.

But how is it in the end? The end is really what matters, isn't it? There are many funerals down here, and we've all wept many tears. But what happens in the end? In Yancey's book, one of the last chapters has this very difficult title: "Is God Silent?" And the writing is hard; the examples hurt. Not everything is resolved. But here's what happens in the end. In one line he writes: "Easter Sunday shows that, in the end, suffering will not triumph."

Can you hold on to that right now? Jesus Himself hung on a cross. Jesus Himself prayed, both in Gethsemane and while nailed to that wooden crossbeam: "Father, take this cup away from Me." And God said "no." God said "No" to the best prayer from the best Pray-er. Jesus felt the horror of the silent God, the darkness, the fog. He felt it like no one ever felt it before. "Why have You forsaken Me?"

Even Jesus cried it out loud: Where is God?

But the Resurrection proves that suffering will end. Death and funerals will end. Terrorism will be obliterated from the universe. Fog will lift. The silent God called forth His own Son with a trumpet and a loud voice. And He's getting ready very soon to do it again.

Can we hold fast until then? A "good soldier" named Darold Bigger had to hang on even when given a battlefield assignment beyond my comprehension. In November 1997 *Ministry* magazine, the lead story, entitled "Journeying Through Personal Grief," was written by this former pastor of the Seventh-day Adventist church at Walla Walla College in Washington.

He was called into the office of the college chaplain one Monday morning and told it was urgent. "Please come straight here." When he got there, he found that John Cress, the chaplain, had also summoned his wife Barbara, from her office. They sat down, and he came right to the point. "I have the worst possible news I could ever share with you," he told them. "Shannon, your daughter, has been killed, murdered in her apartment."

The previous day, Sunday, a man named Anthony had gagged Darold's daughter, tied her to her bed in her Takoma Park, Maryland, apartment, and then murdered her in cold blood. They'd just found her body.

Darold and Barbara and their other daughter, Hilary, had to cope with this news. Shannon was dead. Twenty-five years old, this jewel of their lives had been taken away.

To be honest, Darold Bigger did not experience the "silence of God." He felt God's presence during this ordeal; the reality of his heavenly Father's love and care was something that didn't waver in his mind.

It's one thing to accept the will of God, isn't it? But it's another thing to understand it. No one, really, has satisfactorily explained to us the will of God in permitting the terrorist attacks in New York. "How do we understand something like this?" Billy Graham wondered aloud, in his masterful and sympathetic sermon to the world on September 14. "Why does God allow evil like this to take place? Perhaps that is what you are asking now. You may even be angry at God. I want to assure you that God understands these feelings that you may have." But then he quietly added: "I have been asked hundreds of times in my life why God allows tragedy and suffering. I have to confess that I really do not know the answer totally, even to my own satisfaction. I have to accept, by faith, that God is sovereign, and He's a God of love and mercy and compassion in the midst of suffering."

Obviously Pastor Bigger cannot at this time understand God's will in this incident. There'd be no way humanly possible to know why, when God has a plan, when God is in control, this seemingly random horror had to come into *their* lives.

Philip Yancey's book title *Disappointment With God* has poignant meaning just in those three words. Because even if we love God *in theory,* even if we hang on to the truth that He is good and that He is present, we can't help but be disappointed in Him. God could have saved Shannon Bigger! He's prevented other deaths, and He could have prevented this one. Why didn't He? When random bullets fly, why did He permit this one to reach its target? When floods and fires and earthquakes carve such a seemingly random path through our city, why is our house the one that is destroyed? When other people fortuitously called in sick on that randomly tragic Tuesday morning, but our loved one faithfully went in to the office and met his or her demise, we cannot help but have disappointment with God.

Yancey takes us back once again to the story of Job. Here was a man who got hit hard by Satan . . . and Satan had gotten God's specific permission. "Do what you want with him," God had said, signing off on the request form. "Take anything except his life." And before Job could blink, Satan took his herds, his servants, and all of his children. All Job had left in this entire world was a nagging wife, three foolish friends, and a broken piece of pottery he used to scrape at all the sores Lucifer had put on him.

Now did God provide an explanation? Did He say to Job, "You're My Exhibit A—so please be strong. Heaven is counting on you not to grouch or whine"? No. Not a word. It was as though a dark fog had descended over him; the purposes of heaven were completely hidden. In fact, Yancey writes about that very fog. "The kind of faith God values seems to develop best when everything fuzzes over, when God stays silent, when the fog rolls in" (pp. 242, 243).

In his powerful book *Christianity in Crisis,* author Hank Hanegraaff also writes about this courageous man named Job. Here's how he defines faith: "Faith is trusting God even when you do not understand" (p. 100).

And that was Job. He didn't understand. The evil that happened to him actually *didn't* seem random; in the space of just a few minutes, all these tragedies had completely bowled him over: *Boom—Boom—Boom.* There was a clear pattern of persecution here, and for all Job could know, God was sending this pain to his address. And yet Job trusted in God. He testifies in chapter 13:15: "Though he slay me, yet will I trust in him."

Many times Christians refer to the men and women in the lineup of Hebrews chapter 11 as belonging to the "Faith Hall of Fame." Yancey goes a step further. He puts Job and his faith friends in this category instead: "Survivors of the Fog."

Now there is one more point to pick out of the rubble. In the story of Job, these tragedies were very, very real. His sons and daughters were dead. Those were real people, real flesh-and-blood loved ones—gone. His herds, real cows and sheep, had been destroyed. Trusted servants, also real people with faces and hearts and personalities, had been wiped out. This was the real world, and Job's real world had turned into ashes and sores and tears and death.

The same with Darold and Barbara. The death of their daughter Shannon was painfully real. A real killer had broken in and taken her life. They stood there at the funeral service, and the casket was right in front of them. They couldn't deny the horrible reality of what was happening. The goodness of

God, the reality of heaven, the promises of eternal life—those were the things that must have seemed hidden in the fog for this grieving family—and for Job.

Philip Yancey goes on, though, in *Disappointment With God*, to describe what it is that makes a man like Job or a modern-day sufferer like Pastor Bigger a saint. "Saints become saints by somehow hanging on to the stubborn conviction that things are not as they appear, and that the *unseen* world is as solid and trustworthy as the visible world around them. God deserves trust, even when it looks like the world is caving in."

Does the world of pain around you seem real? It *is* real! But God's world, God's perfect heaven is more real. Can we see it yet? No, we can't. Especially when the fog of a funeral rolls in. This world seems like everything, and what a nightmare world it is too. We watched television on that terrible, devastating Tuesday, wishing desperately that it was *not* real, that, instead, it was a fictional 24-hour M.O.W.—a network movie-of-the-week. The hurts of our planet are very real just now. But here in the Word of God we are told that saints keep their focus on that other world which is *more* real, *more* lasting, *more* enduring.

There is an interesting postscript to the story of Darold and Barbara Bigger's tragedy. The story has not ended, of course. They can't help it; they mark every important date, every birthday, with this stark reminder: "Did it happen before . . . or after . . . June 16, 1996?" They live in the fog, the shadowlands.

But they got an email the very next weekend after the death of Shannon. Doug Clark, a faculty friend, was in the Middle East that weekend. And he sent Darold this message from Jordan: "I didn't go to church in Amman today," he said. "Instead, in Shannon's honor, I've climbed up Mount Nebo . . . to look at the Promised Land."

He stood right there, maybe a few feet away from where Moses stood. And up that high maybe there were clouds. Some fog. But on the other side of the Jordan River was the Promised Land. God's World. A land of resurrections and everlasting reality. And the saint of God hangs in there in the fog, knowing that the Better Land is real, *more* real, eternally more real than the aching loneliness of the moment.

Yes, the day is coming soon when the clouds will lift. The silence of God will end. We'll hear His voice and see His kingdom and know that the reality of His world is just only beginning.

7

Needing a Hiding Place

"I need a place to hide."

Those six words have got to be the theme song of just about every person on this planet. We're all looking for some place to get away, a secret place where we can feel safe and protected.

One national magazine dug out the statistic that in the seven days following the terrorist attacks on New York and Washington, sales of pizza jumped 3.2% from the week before. Why? Because people wanted to hunker down in their own homes and have some "comfort food." St. Patrick's Cathedral in New York had to add six masses a week to accommodate the crowds that wanted to sit in a quiet church and just feel safe.

And even before the violent implosion of those two magnificent towers, this has been the heart cry of a frantic world. Stay-at-home moms with three screaming kids tugging at them would give a hundred dollars just to have one hour of quiet. Men and women in the workplace put in sixty-hour weeks, take work home in a briefcase for the weekend, and have the boss call them up at 10:30 at night with a complaint about missing reports. Executives try to get away for a three-day vacation only to have their beepers and the hotel fax machine break up their solitude.

As a fragmented America and a jittery world recovers from the horrors of September 2001, the book of Psalms kindly points us to "the secret place of hiding with God." Psalm 91 is a beautiful package of metaphors loved by Bible readers around the globe, especially because it speaks about this place of refuge with God and answers the heart cry of the universe.

Do *you* need a place to hide? There's tremendous comfort and hope and strength to be found in the first two verses of Psalm 91: "He who dwells in the secret place of the Most High shall abide under the shadow of the Almighty. I will say of the Lord, 'He is my refuge and my fortress; My God, in Him I will trust' " (NKJV).

I'll grant that if I'm out in the boiling hot desert, I'm glad for a shadow. Finding some shade is high on my priority list. Dr. Alden observes: "To the desert traveler the sun is his fiercest foe and a shady spot a most desired friend." But do we really look to something as fleeting as a *shadow* for protection? For security?

Not usually, no! A shadow isn't really even a thing. It's just a patch of darkness; it might be here right now and gone in five seconds. Shade is nice, but it's kind of ethereal. When we want protection, we want protection that has steel bars and locks and a secret security code.

Ah . . . but this shadow is different! This is *the shadow of the Almighty!*

Where is the secret place of the Most High, then? It's in the shadow of God Himself. Here is an obvious truth that perhaps we forget. A shadow is right next to its source. If we're hiding in the shadow of God, we're standing close to God. We're right next to Him; we're as close as we can get. That's a shadow that can protect! That's a shadow with some muscle to it. In fact, verse 2 describes that "muscle": "I will say of the Lord, 'He is my refuge and my fortress.' "

Now, *fortress*—there's a strong word! Even though it conjures up a picture of a medieval castle built back in the 1500s, you still get a sense of walls that are eight feet thick with a huge gate and a moat and soldiers and security on the inside. Don't we feel wonderfully safe when we stand in church with 300 other believers and sing together "A Mighty Fortress Is Our God"?

Right after the hijackers did their worst, sales of gas masks soared. GasMaskExpress.com sold more than 3,000 of their top-of-the-line model, the Advantage 1000, in just three days, at $200 a pop. Gun sales jumped

20 percent. But wouldn't we rather have God Himself as our Fortress, our protection?

Actually, maybe not. You may be thinking at this very moment: "No, I cannot trust the words to a *song* right now, with all due respect. I need more than a divine shadow. I need a real hiding place. I have real enemies, and they have real bombs—either explosive weapons or cruel words. I've got people at the office who want to do me in. I've got a drinking problem or a methamphetamine addiction that's crushingly real. I'm sorry, but 'Hiding in Jesus' is a little bit trite."

I understand that. I feel it too. At the same time, as just one small fragment of that "cloud of witnesses," let me tell you: closeness to God—standing in the shadow of God through a close daily relationship—*is* a fortress. It *is* protection. This is no mere slogan.

I have Christian friends who have been through painful divorces. The temptation to strike back and to seek revenge must be overpowering at times. But I've watched them stand in the secret hiding place, the shadow at God's feet. I've watched them trust in God for their identity rather than in the security of having a spouse and a father for their children. I've seen discouragement turn into new hope and confidence.

It can work for a president who feels he's under attack. Many believers are thankful to have a leader in the Oval Office who believes in Bible reading. Instead of consulting astrologers or inviting self-help gurus and infomercial talk-show hosts to the White House, America's Commander-in-Chief reads the Psalms. And he can find in those pages his truest identity, his *core,* as a leader ordained by heaven to lead the nation in righteousness.

Do you feel like you're the target of intrigue and office plots? My wife, Lisa, once spent three long years in an office where a coworker was literally out to get her. This was a one-way feud that simmered on the grill every single day of the week, month after month. It wasn't just misery; it was *inescapable* misery.

But the Psalms has an answer for that dilemma as well. "You [God] shall hide them in the secret place of Your presence *from the plots of man; You shall keep them secretly in a pavilion, from the strife of tongues*" (Psalm 31:20, NKJV, emphasis supplied). The attacks may continue; the persecution may go on day and night. Terrorists may concoct new schemes to hurt and kill. But you have a hiding place.

Psychologists sometimes tell their patients to have an imaginary place of peace and safety where they can emotionally retreat during times of stress. Maybe a childhood bedroom where the covers on the bed are fluffy and warm. Perhaps a favorite vacation spot where the brook trickles right past your secluded motel room and the fax machine is broken. Maybe a mountain retreat where the smell of pine trees is heavy in the cool March air.

Sometimes that works. But how much better than an imaginary hiding place is this real fortress we find in the shadow of God's presence! It's available to us all the time; in fact, we can dwell there. It can be our permanent place of refuge. Can you feel the strength of that shadow? The shadow, the quiet power of the shade we find in the presence of God? It is always there for us, even when the temporary shadows of human resources abandon us.

I've always been an enthusiastic fan of the wonderful book *Flee the Captor*, which describes the World War II exploits of the late John Henry Weidner. Time after time, Weidner managed to smuggle desperate people out of the grasp of the Nazis and across the barbed-wire border to freedom. His underground network of friends, the Dutch-Paris organization, helped more than 1,000 Jews, prisoners, and Allied airmen to safety.

A man named Joseph Smit was frantic to get his family out of occupied France. He was willing to pay any price, take any risk, in order to escape with his loved ones. Friends helped to put him in touch with a "passer," a man willing to lead them out. But the costs were exorbitant. By the time Joseph Smit paid the per-person price to this passer, he didn't have much money left.

The journey began, and things went well for the first day or two. They had false papers that seemed to be working; guards at the checkpoints waved them through. Then the passer announced that he was going to go out and get a second person, his partner, who was going to take over the expedition. Joseph hadn't been told this, and it made him extremely fearful. His fears grew when the passer returned and told them that the second agent had fallen through.

However, he had found another man who would take them . . . but only for an additional price. Joseph was outraged and worried that he was being tricked. The whole thing smelled like a con job. But what else could he do? He emptied out every pocket and handed over his last bits of cash to the passer.

"I'll go and get the other man," the guide promised. "He'll be back to get you in a little while."

The second passer never returned.

Imagine the chill of fear that struck into the hearts of the Smit family. Deep in enemy territory with no way out. No safety. Gestapo agents on every street corner and not a friendly face in sight.

Fortunately John Weidner heard of the plight of this desperate family. And so his Dutch-Paris band of volunteers, with no payment at all, led the Smits to the safety of Switzerland. Talk about the comfort of a secret hiding place! Weidner and his friends surely were used by God to provide a shadow of safety to that desperate family.

Psalm 46:1 gives us an additional word picture of this haven of peace: "God is our refuge and strength, an *ever*-present help in trouble" (NIV, emphasis supplied).

Joseph Smit and his family had a guide until the moment of greatest need. All of a sudden, their refuge disappeared, along with all their money. Right when their plight was the most critical, Mr. X vanished on them. And what use is a fair-weather friend who stays around only when the sun is shining?

What kind of God would be there only part of the time? Some days He's on duty, but when you need Him the most, He can't be found. Does the Ruler of the universe sometimes take long coffee breaks, after all?

Praise God we don't have that kind of heavenly Father! God is an *ever-present* help. He's always there! Jesus Christ, in the last verse of Matthew, says to His disciples: "Lo, I am with you alway, even unto the end of the world."

The prophet Elijah had a little bit of fun teasing the prophets of the pagan god Baal, on the top of Mount Carmel. They shouted and screamed and danced around the altar of their sacrifice, trying to get a dial tone to their god. But the line was always busy. Baal's Internet server was down for the entire day. And Elijah couldn't resist. "Come on, guys! Shout louder. Maybe your god is deep in thought, or busy, or traveling, or sleeping. You better try and wake him up."

Finally, when they were all worn down and exhausted, Elijah offered up one simple prayer, just two verses long, and the answer came down instantaneously! (See 1 Kings 18:27-38). Elijah's God was the only ever-present God.

What does that mean to us? We can turn to God at any time. No matter who you are, no matter where you are, He is there for you.

Perhaps you have sung the grand Christian hymn by Isaac Watts, "I Sing the Mighty Power of God." That title fits in beautifully with these two psalms, to be sure. But there's a line in the third verse that goes like this: "There's not a place where we can flee, but God is present there." He really is an ever-present help.

Verse 4 of Psalm 91 says about God our Protector: "He shall cover you with His feathers, and under His wings you shall take refuge" (NKJV). That very comforting metaphor reminds us of the way a hen takes her baby chicks under her wing to provide protection. In fact, Jesus, in the New Testament, used the same word picture to describe His aching-heart love for Israel. " 'O Jerusalem, Jerusalem, you who kill the prophets and stone those sent to you, how often I have longed to gather your children together, as a hen gathers her chicks under her wings, but you were not willing' " (Matthew 23:37, NIV).

Speaking of wings makes us think of a popular song that says, "You are the wind beneath my wings." There's just one problem. Sometimes the wind blows, and sometimes it doesn't blow. The wind can support you for a while, but you wouldn't call the wind an ever-present source of lifting power.

Isn't that the problem with this world? We have friends . . . but you can't depend on them. We have stock market portfolios packed with wonderful tech stocks . . . but you can't count on the market to keep going up. The day the market reopened after the terrorist bombings, a six hundred *billion* dollar mountain vaporized in one trading day.

There's not much we can count on in life except the God of Psalm 46. He's always there. He's an ever-present help. The Living Bible describes Him this way: "God is our refuge and strength, a *tested help* in times of trouble" (emphasis supplied). Yes, as the new praise song shouts out: "Our God is an awesome God."

What does it mean, though, in a spiritual sense, to *dwell* in Him? How does the believer do that?

Well, let's think about what we mean when we say these six words to a guest: *"Please make yourself right at home."* Dr. Tony Evans, who pastors the Oak Cliff Bible Fellowship in Dallas, has an amusing answer to that question in his book *The Victorious Christian Life:*

What you really meant to say was, "Make yourself comfortable in *this room,* since it's the only one in the house that's clean. Don't look behind any closed doors. Don't poke around in the closets. In fact, stay right there in that chair and mind your own business while you're in my house. But, whatever you do, *don't* make yourself at home!"

It's a Bible guarantee that God is always there. But how about us? Do we dart into the cathedral of His presence, into the secret place, for a quick fix of security, and then head back out onto the highway of adventure? Have we really learned to abide in God all the time? Or is the shadow of the Almighty a kind of Christians' motel where the average stay is just one night, until the current rainstorm blows over?

The late Christian writer Marjorie Lewis Lloyd had a favorite anecdote about a man who was desperate to solve a particular problem. "I've tried this and I've tried that," he said to a friend. "I think I've explored just about every option there is. Really, there's nothing left to do now except trust the Lord."

The friend was very sympathetic. "Oh no, has it come to *that?*"

And isn't this indicative of our attitude toward God's hiding place? "Let's not use it until we need it." We think of God as a last resort, a sort of reserve tank. Suddenly, when our security is snatched away, *now* we need God.

We can be grateful that even sporadic users of God's protection often have their prayers answered. God accepts us despite our selfish immaturity and our slow growth away from self-centeredness. But God longs for us to dwell with Him. And He with us! In fact, this invitation to dwell comes *from* Him! Matthew 11:28: " 'Come to Me, all you who labor and are heavy laden, and I will give you rest' " (NKJV).

John 14:23: " 'My Father will love him [God's follower], and We will come to him and make Our home with him' " (NKJV).

Revelation 22:17: "And the Spirit and the bride say, 'Come!' And let him who hears say, 'Come!' And let him who thirsts come. And whoever desires, let him take the water of life freely" (NKJV).

The Bible has many other metaphors that clarify our understanding of this concept of dwelling or abiding. Jesus described Himself as the Vine, with us being the branches. And of course, any branch that's going to live and thrive stays attached to the Vine all the time, not just now and then when the storm clouds gather.

"Pray without ceasing," Christians are told in 1 Thessalonians 5:17. And the verse right before it says: "Rejoice *always.*" Obviously, we can't be on our knees twenty-four hours a day—and we can't be strumming a guitar in Central Park singing gospel praise music nonstop. But can we have an *attitude* of prayer and praise that is nonstop? Can we rejoice at all times in our heart, on both September 9 and 16? That's the kind of dwelling God longs for us to experience.

In a book entitled *In Heavenly Places,* Ellen G. White observes:

> We come to God by special invitation, and He waits to welcome us to His audience chamber. . . . We may be admitted into the closest intimacy and communion with God.
>
> Pray with humble hearts. Seek the Lord often in prayer. In the secret place, alone, the eye sees Jesus and the ear is opened to Jesus. You come forth from the secret place of prayer *to abide under the shadow of the Almighty.* Temptations come, but you press closer and still closer to the side of Jesus and place your hand in His hand. Then you gain a rich experience, resting in His love and rejoicing in His mercy (page 86, emphasis supplied).

She adds this great challenge and promise: "We must abide in Christ and His words must abide in us for His promises to take effect in our lives. What is the defense of the people of God at this time? It is a *living connection* with heaven" (page 348, emphasis supplied). This business of dwelling is a two-way street. Colossians 3:16 says, "Let the word of Christ dwell in you richly" (NKJV).

God wants to be in your life as a 100 percent presence. You abiding in Him and He abiding in you. For some people that's a scary thought. In fact, for all of us this is the real commitment, the final leap that must be made. My childhood missionary friend, Dwight Nelson, pastor at Pioneer Memorial Adventist Church on the campus of Andrews University in Michigan, calls this "radical discipleship."

This is what God wants. He wants all of me and all of you. He wants radical disciples who dwell with Him and love every moment of it. He wants men and women who ask Jesus to affect and infect every part of their lives.

And yes, God "will keep him in perfect peace, whose mind is *stayed* on" Him (Isaiah 26:3, emphasis supplied).

In the end, any God who goes to the trouble to *create* me and then to *redeem* me is going to finally come through and *rescue* me as well. Someone has suggested that those three titles of God, of necessity, must go together: Creator—Redeemer—Rescuer. The first two would be meaningless without the third.

Imagine a little goggle-eyed boy picking out some dream toy in a department store (back in the days when you couldn't charge all your childhood dreams on a VISA card). So he makes payments—a dollar a month, sacrificing, saving—until he's paid the asking price. Wouldn't he then go into the store and claim his prize? After making all the payments, you know he'd want to take that sailboat or that official Red Rider, carbine-action, 200-shot, range-model air rifle or that cherry-red American Flyer bicycle home with him.

The Bible is so full of stories that tell us God is a Rescuer! Daniel in the lions' den. Shadrach, Meshach, and Abednego. Believers never get tired of reading that verse where King Nebuchadnezzar shields his eyes from the glare of the flames and then cries out: " 'I see four men loose, walking in the midst of the fire; and they are not hurt, and the form of the fourth is like the Son of God!' " (Daniel 3:25, NKJV).

Yes, God delivers and He rescues. There's the story of Joseph, who was rescued from the pit, rescued from an overwhelming temptation in Egypt, and rescued from jail—and eventually placed in the seat of honor God had intended for him all along.

The Bible story of Queen Esther and Mordecai is one of overwhelming odds against God's people. Haman, the villain in this Old Testament drama, had a sworn hatred, a vendetta, against them. And so King Xerxes had been tricked into signing a law condemning the Jews to death. The death decree had been sealed by the king, and on the thirteenth day of the twelfth month, it was going to be all over for the followers of the true God.

And then, one by one, a series of unimaginable events falls into place. A long-ago good deed of Mordecai's is discovered, and he's given great honor by the king. It turns out that Esther, the king's beloved bride, is herself Jewish. Three times she's granted a special audience with the king. Then, in a moment of delicious irony, Haman ends up hanged on the very gallows he had constructed for his enemy Mordecai. And the king sends out a second decree, allowing the Jewish nation to defend itself.

Think about it. Long before this moment of danger even loomed, God had already intervened to place Esther on the throne. He wasn't caught flat-footed. Before the crisis happened, God's solution was already locked in. And we have one of the greatest of Old Testament soundbites when Mordecai says to her: " 'Who knows but that you have come to royal position for such a time as this?' " (Esther 4:14, NIV).

I'm convinced that in these last days we're often going to look up in amazement as we see miraculous moments of rescue. We'll see how God set the machinery in place to rescue us and how His plans on our behalf were arranged long before the moment of final battle.

What do you want to believe in today? The devices of the devil or the deliverance of the Lord?

Right now the Lord of the universe is inviting you to choose Him. The evidence is overwhelming that God would like to look after you. He'd like to bring you into close fellowship with Him; He'd like to have you standing, living, dwelling in the shadow of His powerful presence. And, yes, He has a plan to deliver His people. Your name can be placed on the list of His people at this very moment if you just say "Yes."

8

Why Does God Let It Hurt?

Ron Clifford was working in one of the World Trade Center towers when United Flight 175 slammed into it. He didn't find out until later that his own sister, Ruth, and his little four-year-old niece, Juliana, were both on the plane. "Tragically, my sister hit the tower building as my brother was on the ground floor. He's safe now. He's very traumatized," said Ruth's other brother, John. There's a black-and-white picture, a cute mom-and-kid pose in the *Los Angeles Times*. Bright smiles, ponytails, with the likely promise of an ice-cream cone after the photo shoot. And now—devastation.

From the relative safety and isolation that come from not being among those hurting victims, we join each other in asking "Why?" *Why does it have to hurt so bad?* What's the purpose of pain? Why do we have to live on the one planet where cars go hurtling off roads and into trees? Why does our world have to be the place where broken bodies are identified at the morgue? Are there other worlds where hate-filled men deliberately steer jet planes into densely populated buildings as they aim for the highest possible body count? Or is this the only world in God's universe where such things take place? Why *here* . . . and why *us?* Is there a divine purpose to pain? What is it for? Does God send it? Because if He does, if there's some lesson He wants us to learn through cancer or excruciating arthritis or through the tumult of relentless emotional pain, frankly, we think we're willing to learn the lesson without the pain. "Just *tell* us!" we plead. "Stop the punishment. I'll do whatever You want me to do. Just make it stop hurting!"

Long-term, unremitting, unblinking pain is part of our human existence. I have read letters and heard the stories of people who haven't had any relief in decades. Year after year, doctor after doctor, prescription after prescription—it just keeps on coming. Some of these people are the most courageous, brave men and women I've ever encountered. They admit their trials, but end conversations by saying, "I still praise God." Others confess that they honestly don't think they can go on. How much longer can they face a life filled with such pain? Why can't they just die and end the pain?

The Bible tells us that lifelong pain isn't a twenty-first-century phenomenon. In the Gospels there's a story of a woman who'd suffered from a bleeding problem for twelve years. For more than a decade, nothing had worked. In the book of John is told the experience of a crippled man who'd been ill for thirty-eight years. And to make his life experience more painful, he'd been at the edge of the Pool of Siloam, which was alleged to have healing powers. But because he was lame, he couldn't ever be the first one in the water for the miracle moment. What a Catch-22! Imagine being so close to the hope of a cure, and yet his pain and handicap had filled his life for nearly four decades.

The deep theology of why suffering exists and a detailed exploration of the Greek and Hebrew passages that describe human hurting are beyond the scope of this book, and certainly beyond my knowledge. But there are at least two truths that are at the same time simple—and biblically profound.

First of all, God isn't the Author of pain. The world He created was a world without pain, a paradise where the word *suffering* wasn't in the dictionary. The experience of relentless, unending pain was not designed by heaven; it invaded our lives from another agency.

Jesus Himself, in John 10:10, tells us that there has been a thief out there in the darkness. Someone who wants to kill and to destroy and to bring pain. But then He adds this: "I am come that they might have life, and that they might have it more abundantly."

In *Pain: The Gift Nobody Wants,* Dr. Paul Brand shares out of his own childhood a poignant story of pain. Living as a small boy in India, the son of a medical missionary doctor, he was sent at the age of nine to England with his sister Connie. For six long years this young child went to school many thousands of miles away from his parents. Letters from India took months to arrive by steamship (pp. 21, 22).

Then in 1929, his parents announced that they were coming home for a one-year sabbatical. Young teenage Paul looked forward deliriously to the reunion. He could hardly wait. However, just weeks before the big day, a telegram arrived. Father was dead. Malaria and blackwater fever had cut him down at the age of firty-four. And to lose his dad so soon before he was to have seen him again had to be heartbreaking for this young man. Talk about pain! Talk about an unrelenting, never-going-away throbbing of the heart, of endless nights staring out of the bedroom window missing your dad.

And Dr. Brand writes about the foolish things people said to him: "Your father was a wonderful man, too good for this world." *But what about the rest of us—does that mean we're not good enough?*

"God needed him in heaven more than we need him on earth." *No! I haven't seen Dad in six years. I need my dad!*

"His work was finished here." *That can't be true! The church is barely beginning, and the medical work is growing. Who will care for the hill people now? And what about my mother?*

"It's for the best." *How, tell me HOW, can it POSSIBLY be best?* (p.272).

And for a while this struggling teenager thought that maybe it was *his* fault. God was punishing him. Or maybe punishing his mother. Guilt began to consume the family.

Brand then says to his reading audience: "This is not a book of theology. . . . Yet I have seen so much harm caused by guilt over this one issue that I would be remiss if I did not mention it as a pain *intensifier*. Hundreds of patients I have treated—Muslim, Hindu, Jewish, and Christian— have tormented themselves with questions of guilt and punishment. What have I done wrong? Why me? What is God trying to tell me? Why do I deserve this fate?"

Dr. Brand and coauthor Philip Yancey go on to assert that human pain and suffering are *not* sent as a punishment. "If God is using human suffering," they write, "He certainly has picked an obscure way to communicate His displeasure. The most basic fact about punishment is that it only works if the person knows the reason for it. It does absolute harm, not good, to punish a child unless the child understands why he or she is being punished. Yet most patients I have treated feel mainly confused, not chastened, by suffering" (pp. 272, 273).

Many were stunned by that bold assertion a television minister made after the September 11 attacks, suggesting that God had allowed these attacks because of the work of civil-liberties groups, abortion-rights supporters, homosexual activists, and feminists. Thankfully, the accusation brought this quick rejoinder from Wayne Pederson, chairman of the National Religious Broadcasters:

> God has no doubt used the tragic events of the past week to cause our nation and the church to seek His face as never before. The Old Testament gives many examples of how God allowed tragedy to bring His people back to Himself. *God doesn't cause evil to happen.* He allows man to make choices. Often man chooses evil actions that hurt innocent lives. But God is not surprised by this. God is a master at turning tragedy into triumph. His plan will ultimately prevail to His glory (fax to NRB membership, Sept. 18, 2001).

In the Bible, as Brand and Yancey point out, those who received divine punishment in the Bible generally knew why! When the ten plagues fell on the land of Egypt, the disobedient Egyptians knew why they were coming. Prophets told of upcoming hardships because of apostasy. But in the book of Job, the all-time classic story of suffering , Job was *not* being punished. God Himself said Job was blameless and upright, a man who feared God and shunned evil (pp. 273, 3–5).

If you're hurting today, I cannot blithely say that I feel your pain, but God does. In the book of Daniel, where the three brave young men were tossed into the fiery furnace, that wasn't God's fire. He didn't light it or stoke the flames. But in that terrible moment, *He was there* with His three children.

Are we ever blessed by being in the fiery furnace of trials and temptations? "God uses pain," is how Wayne Pederson of NRB puts it. "He uses [or permits] it to draw us back to Himself" (fax 9/18/10). What would happen if we never encountered the hard bumps of reality?

Dr. Brand tells the heartbreaking story of a baby girl named Tonya. This small child, just seventeen or eighteen months old, had a rare medical problem described as "congenital indifference to pain." Her mother first discovered it when she came into the baby's room one day and found her tiny daughter happily fingerpainting red swirls all over the white plastic sheet in the playpen. To her horror, the mother discovered that her daughter had bitten off the tip of her own finger and was playing in the blood. Apparently, she simply did not feel pain—ever! Cuts and bruises and bites and spankings were completely ineffective as danger signals. Nothing hurt, and it got to the point where the parents simply couldn't protect Tonya from herself. In fact, this tiny child discovered that she could emotionally blackmail her own parents; if she misbehaved and they threatened anything, she would simply raise a finger to her mouth as though about to bite it, and they would cave in (p. 65).

It's a wrenching medical story, and it demonstrates the truth of Dr. Brand's assertion that at times pain can actually be one of life's greatest blessings. Amazingly, this best-selling author describes himself as a "career lobbyist for pain." Because in his many long years as a doctor among lepers, he experienced firsthand the truth that pain is often a lifesaver.

The personal stories he shares are incredible. But the dramatic thread of challenge all through the pages of his book has to do with helping people who simply don't feel pain. These sufferers of leprosy, Hansen's Disease, as it's often called today, don't have sensations that warn them of danger. They burn fingers and don't know it. They walk on sensitive sore spots, even raw places, on their feet, and don't know to shift their weight to protect themselves. Brand writes about seeing lepers walking along briskly, almost jogging . . . on bleeding stumps with the bones sticking through. And they simply didn't know to stop. The element of pain was not there to protect them.

And as the story develops, Brand and Yancey compellingly relate how our bodies reveal what is actually a Creator's loving design. Did you know, for example, that your eye is a thousand times more sensitive to pain than the sole of your foot? Which makes sense, of course. With the eye being a tool of vision, it needs to be transparent, which limits the number of opaque blood vessels. And any intruder—a speck of dust, a fist coming toward it—invokes an immediate and reflexive act of protection. Your two eyeballs have a hair-trigger sensitivity to pain and a hair-trigger blink mechanism to keep pain out.

On the other hand, the soles of your feet are tough enough to withstand a lot more pain. Two hundred grams per square millimeter of pressure, as opposed to two tenths of a gram on the eyeball. And that's built in to our human design! We're made to feel the right levels of pain in order to protect ourselves.

"The beauty of pain," Dr. Brand writes, "is that it lets you know right away when you are harming yourself." Then he adds:

> Pain, my body's way of alerting me to danger, will use whatever volume level is necessary to grab my attention. It was their very deafness to this chorus of messages that caused my leprosy patients to destroy themselves. They missed the 'shouts' of pain, leading to the direct injuries that I treated every day. And they also missed the whispers of pain, the dangers of the ordinary that come from constant or repetitive stress (p. 177).

And God intends for us to look beyond the warnings of physical pain, the signals it sends, and seek the promise of eternity with Him. God often uses spiritual pain as a warning of upcoming danger in the realm of the soul. The first bits of carelessness begin to manifest themselves in your life in the area of personal devotions, for example. You used to spend time with God each day, but for the last month now you've kind of put it off. Things were hard at the office, and you just didn't get around to having any meaningful time of Bible study and prayer. And all at once, you felt the twinge of guilt. You missed it! Or a temper flare-up reminded you that things were different inside your heart. The soft tenderness had developed a bit of a crust.

A recent contemporary Christian song has God crying out: "I miss my time with you." ("I Miss the Way," from *i2 [EYE]* album, Michael W. Smith and Wayne Kirkpatrick, O' Ryan Music, Inc. [ASCAP], © 1988.) And perhaps there's a kind of pain in your life that is serving as a jolt. Wake up! Smell the coffee! Something is wrong in your prayer closet; it's been empty far too long.

A wise God knows our spiritual pain threshold and sends just the signal we need. For some sensitive Christians, just the slightest tremor of conscience will send them to their knees. Some of the rest of us, more hardened and foolish, like the sole of Huckleberry Finn's bare foot, have needed more drastic pain signals. And a loving God allows the necessary pain, that corrective measure, to bring us back to Him.

But then comes the oh-so-human temptation to try to block out the pains of life, which is sometimes appropriate. And yet, both in the physical and spiritual arenas, our bottles of aspirin and sore-muscle ointments can be deadly deceptions.

Pain relief in the United States is now a $63-*billion*-a-year industry, says Brand; Americans, who represent 5 percent of the world's population, consume 50 percent of its manufactured drugs. And he quotes a TV commercial line that you've probably heard: "I haven't got time for the pain."

The good doctor who writes this book expresses a longing for just one magazine advertisement or commercial that at least acknowledges some benefit to pain. He writes:

> I wish they would say, "First, *listen* to your pain. It is your own body talking to you." It may be trying to tell you that you are violating your brain with tension, your ears with loudness, your eyes with constant television, your stomach with unhealthy food, your lungs with cancer-producing pollutants. Listen carefully to the message of pain before I give you something to relieve those symptoms. I can help with the symptoms, but *you* must address the cause (p. 188).

We sometimes try to block out spiritual symptoms, don't we? We ask the coach of the team to rub some pain-killing liniment on our soul so that we can play the entire second half without feeling pain. And there are many ways to drown out the twinges of sin. Busy-ness and a louder TV and a more frantic social life *or even more work at church* . . . they all mask the pain, the still, small voice of the conscience. They all block out the pain that a loving God, the Great Physician, may be trying to use right now as a signal to your heart.

This is not to say that all pain is good—either in the world of medicine or the spirit either. Even Jesus our Savior underwent heartaches and excruciating pain that can only be described as horror, a price paid for our sins. But the book of Hebrews also says that Jesus learned obedience through suffering (see Hebrews 5:8), and perhaps God is calling us to do the same.

After a lifetime of helping people whose lives were tragically destroyed because they couldn't feel pain, and after many long years of helping people compensate for that congenital handicap, Dr. Paul Brand's own daughter had a baby boy. His first grandson. And of course, Grandpa had to personally check to make sure that there were ten fingers and ten toes and that the spine was in line and all the rest. But there was one test that Dr. Brand wanted to do on little Daniel . . . and he waited until Mom was in the other room.

With an ordinary straight pin, this loving physician gave that infant boy a healthy poke in one finger. The baby yanked his hand back, looked at the injured finger, and then at Grandpa Brand—no doubt a look of severe disapproval.

And do you know what this Christian physician did? He held that little grandson close to his heart and prayed a prayer of thanksgiving to God, praising the Creator for the intricate mechanisms that caused pain and that would provide this small baby with protection throughout his life. "Previously I had thought of pain as a blemish in creation," he wrote. "God's one great mistake. . . . Now pain stands out as an extraordinary feat of engineering valuable beyond measure" (pp. 196,197,62).

Brand and other physicians who have studied the psychological effects of pain have all discovered one central truth: human beings are created to survive pain by fellowship and human contact. It is much more difficult—in fact, almost impossible—to endure pain all by yourself.

One of the great survival stories is the saga of Pastor Noble Alexander, prisoner in the Cuban system for twenty-two long years. His story, *I Will Die Free,* (Pacific Press, 1991) is an exciting, almost unbelievable description of a man enduring and triumphing over pain.

This brave preacher endured unimaginable kinds of torture in Castro's prisons. He survived months of time holed up in "the box." The so-called water torture, where he was held underneath ice-cold water over and over until within seconds of death. Stabbings and shootings and months of starvation and marathon interrogation sessions where he was subjected to agonizing, unrelenting pain inflicted by cruel men.

But there were two things that enabled Noble Alexander to survive for those twenty-two years. First of all, he was a Christian. All his life he'd trusted in Jesus Christ for sustaining power during the difficult times of life in Cuba. When the prison guards' guns were aimed at his head or when he spent hours and days standing in a box with his heels digging into the jagged spikes deliberately placed there, he could only call on God for the will to survive. He had nowhere else to turn, but he did have that.

But there was a second secret that kept this man going. And that was the gift of *community*. As Noble found himself thrust into these horrific dungeons with other men, a group will began to emerge. These inmates started to coalesce into a band, a united force of human determination. They started churches, with Noble dubbed as "The Pastor." They organized prayer cells, prayer meetings, even a makeshift university, where the educated among them would train the others in college-level course work.

But above all, they developed this community motto: "We will die free!" They would defeat Castro by surviving. True, he and his followers could shoot them or starve them or beat them to death. But the prisoners would not surrender their spirit; they would not sign papers admitting their so-called crimes against the state. They would not back down and accept the authority of the tyrant who was trying to break their wills.

And so often during the twenty-two years, when one man was being tortured and experiencing the excruciating pain, the others would rally to his side. "Hang in there, man!" Noble would hear from outside his solitary confinement. "We will die free!" When his own wife sold out to the communists and came to the prison to flaunt her new freedom and rub his face in the fact of his divorce, it was the support of the other men that gave him the emotional strength to keep on living.

Pain is such a terrible thing, and it's made more terrible when experienced alone. When you hurt all by yourself—and nobody else understands or even knows about it—that's hard. There's a classic line from *Romeo and Juliet:* "He jests at scars that never felt a wound."

With those Shakespearian words ringing in our minds, we can be— like Noble Alexander—thankful for two things when enduring pain. First of all, be grateful for Jesus. Not just because we can call on Him, but because He is a Savior who knows and understands our pain. He doesn't "jest at my scars" and shrug at the sight of my whimpering. No, Jesus is Immanuel—"God With Us"—in our suffering.

Hebrews 4:15 says this about Jesus Christ: "We do not have a high priest who is unable to sympathize with our weaknesses, but we have one who has been tempted in every way, just as we are—yet was without sin" (NIV).

As Pastor Alexander experienced the agony of that row of nails digging into his flesh, he remembered that Jesus felt nails too. When an inmate was stabbed and then dragged away bleeding, the men recalled that Christ was stabbed at Calvary. When Noble felt the loneliness of knowing his family had abandoned him, he could recall the Gethsemane scene, where Christ's own disciples betrayed and denied Him. Jesus is part of our community of pain; in fact, He's our Leader in surviving the hard trail of this world.

Tim Stafford writes:

> Those who embrace suffering as part of their calling in Christ remain blind to its purpose. They may not see how their battle affects the larger battle. They can see, nonetheless, that bravery and obedience are called for, just as for a soldier in battle. As those on Jesus' side, suffering as His servants, they may catch a glimpse of Him walking ahead, fighting for them *Knowing the Face of God,* (p. 235).

That's comforting imagery, to catch a glimpse of Jesus on the pathway ahead of us, His sword drawn and ready for battle. To know that He's with us in the fiery furnace of our pain.

But we can also be thankful for community, for the shared element of suffering. True, we often suffer alone, even in the Body of Christ—but that's not how it should be. We are commanded to bear one another's burdens (see Galatians 6:2) and share each person's pain.

A flight attendant on Delta Airlines Flight 15 from Frankfurt to Atlanta, Georgia, describes her very personal experience. The date on the flight manifest was 9/11/01, and about five hours out of Frankfurt, the plane did an abrupt right-hand turn and landed at Gander, Newfoundland. All flights into the United States, passengers were told, had been cancelled.

Soon there were fifty-three huge airplanes parked on the tarmac at this small airport. And the passengers of this particular Delta jet ended up staying in that plane from 12:30 in the afternoon until 10:30 the following morning. Passengers included, by the way, a woman in her thirty-third week of pregnancy.

Not surprisingly, a spirit of community developed on board, as passengers cared for one another. After twenty-two long hours, they finally exited the aircraft and were taken into this small town of Gander, population 10,400. There was *one hotel* in town. But all towns within a 75-kilometer radius closed high schools, meeting halls, and lodges, and converted them into mini-hotels for the "plane people." (A family offered a private room in their home to the pregnant woman.) All the passengers from this particular flight ended up in the small town of Lewisporte. Everyone got free food; laundromats gave all passengers tokens. Local townspeople took visitors on excursions of lakes and harbors.

Finally, on Friday morning, three days after the New York tragedy, the passengers were taken back to the airport and sent on their way. And this flight attendant confesses in amazement: "Our flight back to Atlanta looked like a party flight. We simply stayed out of their way. The passengers had totally bonded and they were calling each other by their first names, exchanging phone numbers, addresses, and e-mail addresses."

Then a business-class passenger approached this particular attendant and asked if he could "borrow" the plane's PA system to make an announcement. That would be strictly against Delta policy, of course, but somehow she felt compelled to grant him that privilege. The gentleman, a physician, reminded everyone of the hospitality they had just experienced, the *community*, the sharing of hurts and pain. "I'm going to start a trust fund," he then declared, "for the people of Lewisporte." The Delta 15 Fund would go to provide college scholarships for the teenagers of that town, and he offered to personally match whatever amount the passengers chose to donate. Before the plane touched down at Hartsfield International Airport, there was fifteen thousand dollars in the hat.

Tim Stafford comments:

> It is remarkable how many relationships can be traced back to *shared misery*. We have, to name a few examples, married couples who cheerfully remember their first poverty-stricken years together; we have war buddies wounded by the same shell; we have cancer victims who shared the same hospital room. Even friendships made in school often form around the shared loneliness and frustration of growing up. . . . Here at last is someone who knows what it was like (ibid., p. 229).

Even with the benefits of *community*, though, there do come those moments when we have to sit alone, look in the mirror, and say: "This hurts. And what does it mean?" The old adage, "Suffering builds character," continues to be three of the most unpopular words in the world, right up there with "Eat your spinach; it's good for you."

An old Peanuts® cartoon strip from "way back when" has Charlie Brown and his baseball team losing yet again. And, of course, there have been innumerable line drives of the kind that cause pitcher Charlie Brown to go flying off the mound, his hat and glove and even his clothes sailing in all directions.

On the way home he complains to one of the other characters. Why has the team lost again? Five million to nothing! And this is the eightieth loss in a row! Nobody can hit. He's got a beagle for a shortstop. Lucy certainly doesn't try very hard out there in center field. Etc. Etc. And Charlie Brown, whose secret unfulfilled ambition has always been to be called "Flash" is one dejected athlete.

Finally Linus speaks up with a casual shrug. "Look at it this way, Charlie Brown. You learn more from losing than you do from winning."

Well, that's exactly what Charlie Brown does not want to hear. Turning on him in sorrow and rage, he knocks him right over with a shriek: "THAT MAKES ME THE SMARTEST PERSON IN THE WORLD!"

We can sympathize with our friend Charlie Brown, but we have to admit that the late Christian cartoonist Charles Shultz must have been reading his Bible faithfully—especially the book of Romans where the apostle Paul writes: "We rejoice in our sufferings, because we know that suffering produces perseverance; perseverance, character; and character, hope" (5:4, NIV).

The *NIV Study Bible* text notes add: "A Christian *can* rejoice in suffering because he knows that it is not meaningless. Part of God's purpose is to produce character in His children." Still, the son or daughter of God has an advantage in being able to trust that God does have an ultimate purpose in his or her life.

Are you suffering today? Is pain a part of your daily life? Did the events of September 11, 2001, scar you in ways that the rest of the world doesn't understand? Pain may be firmly in your path at this moment; it's part and parcel of your future, and frankly, you can't see if there's anything *else* in your future. "How can I possibly go on?" you wonder. Especially when the pain is simply *there*. It's undeserved. It's a random attacker. There's no reason it's part of your life except for the fact that we live in a cruel, sin-soaked world. You don't have a lesson to learn; you're simply on the enemy's hit list. What perspective can you possibly adopt that will see you through this endless valley of shadows?

All we can say then is that we suffer for the sake of Christ. Maybe there's nothing else, no other reason. But the Bible tells us that there's nobleness and reward in being a fellow sufferer with Jesus Christ. He suffered too—and you and I, as part of His family, may well have a heavy cross to bear.

Philippians 1:29 makes that very statement: "It has been granted to you on behalf of Christ not only to believe on him, but also to suffer for him" (NIV).

The book of Acts says that the first Christian apostles left the Sanhedrin *rejoicing that they were counted worthy to suffer shame for [Jesus'] name"* (Acts 5:41, NKJV, italics supplied).

That willingness, that spirit of rejoicing in the midst of suffering, is largely why the infant Christian church survived. There was incredible pain and persecution for those first followers of Christ. Beatings and crucifixions and lions and the agony of families torn apart, either by the wild beasts of Rome or by the spiritual splits this new faith caused. And what impact did all the flowing blood have? Louis Bouyer writes: "The importance of martyrdom in the spirituality of the early Church would be difficult to exaggerate. . . . After the elements of the New Testament, certainly no other factor has had more influence in constituting Christian spirituality."

But even more than character development is the simple truth that, through all that comes our way, Jesus is there. In your darkest hour, the Son of God stands by your side. He really and truly is *there with you;* "Immanuel," "God with us."

C. S. Lewis wrote a letter to an American friend just a few months before his own death. Here is what he said about relaxing in Jesus' arms:

> Remember, though we struggle against things because we are afraid of them, it is often the other way around—we get afraid *because* we struggle. Are you struggling, resisting? Don't you think Our Lord says to you, "Peace, child, peace. Relax. Let go. Underneath you are the everlasting arms. Let go, I will catch you. Do you trust Me so little?" (Letters to an American Lady, p.114).

Right now in the stillness of your own heartaches, can you feel those everlasting arms?

9

I Like It in This Fiery Furnace!

It was probably the hardest shopping trip of his life. Richard and his wife, Mildred, had a list of things to buy, things he could take along on this unique outing. "Six undershirts, 6 briefs, 1 belt, 1 collared shirt, 1 pair of dress slacks, 1 pair of leather sole shoes or boots, 2 pairs of socks, 1 sweatsuit, 1 tennis racket, 4 tennis balls, 4 racket balls, 1 pair of sneakers."

Does it sound like Richard is off to Club Med? Actually, Pastor Richard Dortch was putting into his suitcase the things the United States Marshal Service had told him he could bring into prison. Because he, inmate #07423-058, soon to be a federal prisoner for his role in the Jim Bakker PTL scandal, was packing up to enter Eglin Prison in Florida.

There was one more thing on the vacation list. "One single-edge razor." Electric razors were forbidden in a federal prison, because clever inmates knew how to re-wire electrical devices for unauthorized purposes. So at 9:30 at night, the evening before he was to go to jail, his last night of freedom, Richard and Mildred Dortch drove to a K-Mart to buy a single-edge razor.

In his book, *Integrity: How I Lost It, and My Journey Back,* Dortch writes from the bottom of his heart about how it felt to know that he, a Christian minister, ordained in the Assembly of God denomination, was about to go to jail like a common crook. There was shame and embarrassment involved, certainly. He'd let down his family, his friends, his ministry partners. But he had the same fears as any other normal person about prison. He feared the loneliness, the isolation, the danger. Would he be stabbed? Raped? Persecuted for being such a high-profile, wealthy inmate next to the guys who had perhaps robbed K-Mart for a razor? He knew he was going to be classified with a CIM rating: Central Inmate Monitoring because he was a well-known personality, subject to physical attack.

And there was more to worry about. "When you are there [in prison] for a sentence of three years or more," he writes, "there is an eighty percent chance that you will leave divorced." Richard Dortch was facing an eight-year sentence. Would Mildred still be there when he got out?

He writes about how it felt to know that he had only a week of freedom left. February 2, 1990, was seven days away. Then six. Five. *Five days, and I'll be in prison.* He was fifty-eight years old and suffered from Crohn's disease, which sometimes caused him excruciating pain. Would he survive these years in federal lockup?

A story like that takes us right into the heat and the flames of our own theme park of this chapter: the fiery furnace. The place of trials and pain. The place where Shadrach, Meshach, and Abednego found themselves— and sometimes you and I find ourselves there too.

In 1Peter, we find these difficult words: "In this you greatly rejoice, though now for a little while you may have to suffer grief in all kinds of trials." Rejoice? Even when you are suffering? It's hot in that fiery furnace, so rejoice. It's lonely there in Eglin Prison, Richard Dortch, so rejoice and be glad. It's depressing in that cancer ward, so rejoice. You now have to make it alone in this world, Gabrielle Hoffman, because your husband, Steve, lost his life in the World Trade Center attack. His income from Cantor Fitzgerald is gone, and you have to pay the $3000-a-month mortgage all by yourself. And raise your five-year-old, Madeline, all by yourself. The stillness of death tears at your heart as you stand by the grave of your beloved spouse, there in the cemetery after the other mourners have all gone home, so rejoice and be glad. Does the Bible really mean this? Is it wonderful to be in that fiery furnace?

You might be tempted to say, "Sure, it's not bad in the furnace—as long as you don't burn up." But a lot of Christians have gotten burned in the fire. The person we love the most in all this world does die. Cancer does strike unexpectedly, and Christians die in the same proportionate numbers as non-Christians. Michael Baksh, in his mid-thirties, was an active member of the Church of the Advent Hope in Upper Manhattan, the chairperson of his church board. Tuesday, September 11, was *his first day on the job* at the World Trade Center, Tower 2. He died on his first morning of work there, leaving behind a wife and two kids.

All Christians draw courage and inspiration by this old Bible story about the three young men in a fiery furnace. Who can calculate the positive good that has come to Richard Dortch's ministry, his ability to share Christ with others, now that he's been to prison and back?

Dortch's son, Rich, said to him right at the time of sentencing, in one of his father's lowest moments of despair: "Dad, if you and Mom were in a missionary service, and a call was given to go to a mission field where there were people who needed help, you would respond. You would probably be the first ones on your feet. Look at this as a mission field, and you'll be all right" (pp. 266–268).

Consider the results. Today Richard Dortch is the president of a ministry called Life Challenge, Inc., which helps professional men and women in times of crisis. Imagine what it means to would-be counselees to know that the man helping them has been through this fire himself! They know he can relate; they know he understands the pressures they face. They know his testimony; his confession about the power of Jesus Christ to restore is real. Just as the influence of Shadrach, Meshach, and Abednego spread throughout Babylon when they emerged unscathed from that furnace, this experience of incarceration has empowered Richard Dortch's ministry in a way no one could ever envision.

Well, all of this might have worked out better for Richard Dortch than you think it is working out for you. He was paroled in less than a year and a half, and you might still be rotting away in a jail cell, or at least the prison of your own secret pain. But jot down this final thought from a man God saw through to the other side. "Faith is not determined," Dortch writes, "by winning or losing." Or by getting paroled or not getting paroled, we might add. Or by sickness or health, prosperity or adversity, death or life. "But by simply resting in the plan God has for us" (p. 283).

Sometimes we rest. Sometimes we rejoice. Sometimes we wait. But if God is with us, we never have to wonder. C. S. Lewis writes to that American lady he never met: "Beneath are the everlasting arms, even when it doesn't feel at all like it" (p. 48).

Speaking of those everlasting arms and God's promise to be an ever-present help in times of trouble, there's a rendering of the ancient Shadrach, Meshach, and Abednego tale that's delightfully unique. As this particular preacher—a rather excitable man of the cloth—was telling the story, God up in heaven was very much concerned. "My three boys are down there in that fire," He cried, His voice echoing throughout Paradise. "My boys are in danger; they're in the flames." And all the angels gathered around, great distress on their faces.

God rose up from His throne, love and worry written on His face. "We cannot let those three boys perish in the fires of that Nebuchadnezzar! Never! I must do something to help My boys." And He looked around. "Where's such-and-such angel?" And He named one of the kingdom's most mighty angel warriors, a being with a wonderful spirit, a rescuing heart. "Where's that angel?" And the summoned angel stepped forward.

"How long will it take you to travel down to that little planet, earth, that tiny place, that plain of Dura?" God asked. "How long to make the trip . . . because My boys are in such danger?" And the angel responded immediately. "Father, I can be there in five minutes."

"Five minutes!" And God was in despair. "In five minutes, they'll be gone. Nothing but ashes. Five minutes is far too long!" And He turned in the other direction. "Give me Gabriel then! Gabriel, My greatest archangel. Gabriel, the speediest of all My forces." Well, Gabriel was instantly standing front and center. And God leaned forward, more anxious than ever because time was running out. "Gabriel, My best angel, My commanding angel, how long to wing your way down to Shadrach, Meshach, and Abednego?" And Gabriel, eager to charge the gates of Babylon, his wings already fluttering, warming up, told the Father: "Two minutes."

"Two minutes!" And God paced in frustration. "We can't wait another two minutes! And the flames are so hot! My boys are in grave danger."

So God went to the final option. "I'll send My own Son! That's what I'll do! Jesus, My only Son, will make the journey. Who can travel to earth more quickly than My only begotten Son?" So He cried out: "Jesus! Son! Quickly! Our children are in the flames! Two minutes is too long to wait! Hurry! Jesus, Son, where are You?" And the angels looked around the courtroom of heaven; they gazed high and low. They looked in every corner. But they didn't see Jesus anywhere. Where could He be? And the Father cried out again: "Jesus, we have no time to spare! My Son, where are You?"

And from far, far below, from clear down on that distant planet, that faraway speck in the universe where a king named Nebuchadnezzar had lit his little fire, came the shout of reply: "Don't worry, Dad, I'm already down here!"

Well, we could almost rest our case right here! Because this is *the* lesson of Daniel 3. There are trials and tribulations that are red-hot; they're life-threatening. In fact, sometimes they don't just threaten a believer's life, they take it. But the Son of God, that swiftest of ambassadors, is the fourth Person in the flames.

When trials hit, believers in Christ can know that Jesus is with them. Just as literally as this fourth Man was standing there in the fire, protecting His three friends, the resurrected Jesus—through the presence of the Holy Spirit—is actually there with you. He's "In This Very Room," as the Christian song suggests.

The story of the three faithful Hebrews in the fiery furnace seems to confirm the promise found in Isaiah 43:2. " 'When you pass through the waters, I will be with you; and through the rivers, they shall not overflow you. When you walk through the fire, you shall not be burned, nor shall the flame scorch you' " (NKJV).

Those are beautiful words, but a courtroom objection may be welling up in your throat. It's there in mine as well. "Wait a minute!" we cry out. "Shadrach, Meshach, and Abednego didn't get burned—but John Huss did! My nephew did. A little girl who attended the local grade school drowned just last week; despite what the Bible said, the waters *did* pass over her. A modern-day reading of this verse might say this: "When you climb on board a 767 plane, it will never crash. Hijackers will be stopped at the gate, apprehended in the parking lot." And yet in one fiery morning, four planes went down with Christians on board. So it's true that in a sin-sick world, the promise of Isaiah 43:2 is not an ironclad, 100-percent-sure guarantee. Water drowns and flames burn and cancer kills. But two facts are incontrovertible.

First of all, there are five words that *are* ironclad. "I will be with you." A Bible hero named Peter was in prison, and God was with him. God gave him a Monopoly card that said: "Get out of jail free." John the Baptist was in prison, and God was with him too. Even so, he died—*temporarily*. The great apostle Paul was stoned, but God was with him and spared him. The great deacon Stephen was stoned, and God was with him too. But he died—*temporarily*.

All through these sixty-six books, the Old and the New Testament, we're always promised two things. God is present in our trials. And our trials, even if they lead to death, are temporary. The trials will be temporary, and the death will be very temporary. The Old Testament promises us in the book of Hosea: " 'I will ransom them from the power of the grave; I will redeem them from death. Where, O death, are your plagues? Where, O grave, is your destruction?' " (Hosea 13:14, NIV). And the New Testament echoes the same promise in 1 Corinthians 15:55. Paul himself agrees that death is not to be feared. Dying or not dying is not a great issue for the Christian because Jesus conquered death. Because Jesus is with us in our trials. Because Jesus made death so temporary. He's with us; that's the main thing. Some people die in the flames; others don't—but He's with them all.

And today God is as concerned about the flames surrounding you, the problems, the mounting bills, the looming divorce. "That's My child. Come on, Heaven, let's swing into action! Come on, brigades, let's fire up the engines!" Does Heaven always rescue? No. But it always travels to the spot. Holy angels, and even Jesus Himself—through the presence of the Holy Spirit—join you in your darkest moment.

The apostle Paul writes about all of the bad things that had happened to him; in fact, he almost brags about his laundry list of lamentable occurrences. Beatings and whippings and prison and hunger and shipwrecks (see 2 Corinthians 11:24-28). But he praises God! He celebrates God's presence. What's the secret? Paul himself answers on behalf of all of us. Just five words from Philippians 3:20: "Our citizenship is in heaven" (NKJV).

Someone's house burns down. That's bad news. But his citizenship is in heaven. Someone's body is wracked with pain and disease; it's terminal for sure. But a glorified new body is promised because his citizenship is in heaven. Someone's spouse has left her; she is lonely, trying to pay the rent. But God promises her that she won't be lonely in a well-populated better land; her citizenship is in heaven. LeRoy Homer was a copilot on United Airlines Flight 93, which crashed in western Pennsylvania on September 11. His widow, Melodie, continues to faithfully attend the Mt. Holly English Church in New Jersey. Her citizenship is in heaven.

That's why Jesus, who loves us so much, can give that seemingly impossible encouragement to the man or woman enduring suffering and trials. "Rejoice and be glad."

But beyond the biblical injunction to "rejoice," are there practical steps the believer can take when the flames of hardship are licking at his ankles? It hardly seems decorous to draw theology from Peanuts® cartoon strips in two successive chapters, but a lot of homespun biblical wisdom was illustrated by the cartoonist's pen of the late Charles Schultz. And in one archived adventure, Charlie Brown, the poor, persecuted misfit who is always the butt of jokes, the object of scorn, recipient of Lucy Van Pelt's sarcasm, finally has had enough. From a good safe distance, he screams at his tormenters the old line: "Sticks and stones may break my bones, but words can never hurt me!"

Two seconds later, in the last frame, a stick comes flying through the air, and it *clonks* Charlie Brown right on the head. So he gets it both ways.

But that old expression, which turned out to be no defense for young Charlie Brown, isn't for us either. "Words can never hurt me"? You and I both know that those five words are among the most *un*true in the English language. Every hour of every day, words are unleashed that cut to the heart, that wound, that even kill.

There was a cartoon in the Fall 1998 issue of *Leadership,* a Christian magazine for pastors. And please don't get the idea that cartoons are the only thing I ever read for sermon preparation. But the punch line was this: "You know, pastor, that you're in trouble when the church's voice mail system includes an option that says, 'To complain about Sunday's sermon, press three' " (p. 13).

In Matthew 5, Jesus also talks about rejoicing when trials come, when we're persecuted. He doesn't simply address the dilemma of people in fiery furnaces, or Christians who are thrown to the roaring lions or led out to the gallows to be hanged. No, Jesus Christ talks even more about the kind of persecution most of us encounter; He talks specifically about *words*: " 'Blessed are you when people insult you, persecute you and falsely say all kinds of evil against you because of me' " (verse 11, NIV). And then Jesus adds the promise and an explanation: " 'Rejoice and be glad, because great is your reward in heaven, for in the same way they persecuted the prophets who were before you' " (verse 12, NIV).

So if your trial and suffering is one of bearing insults, Jesus gives you comfort. If people lie about you, He promises you that He's got a reward for you, to make up for it all. If Charlie Brown is saved in God's kingdom, he can know that God will not only bind up that bruise on his head, but also heal his heart for all the times that Lucy called him "you blockhead," for all of the insults he endured when his team lost in baseball.

However, we should also notice three very important words tucked away in verse 11. " 'Blessed are you when people insult you, persecute you and falsely say all kinds of evil against you *because of me*' " (emphasis supplied).

It's vital to realize that Jesus isn't really talking about baseball games or about celebrity guests who get insulted on the Howard Stern radio show. No, these are trials and sufferings—verbal cruelty—that men and women experience because of their faith. Because they witness to a relationship with Jesus. The prophet Isaiah must have been one of those preachers who had a lot of parishioners hit "three" on his voicemail to complain about sermons, because he writes in chapter 51: " 'Hear me, you who know what is right, you people who have my law in your hearts.' " So this command is written to a believer: " 'Do not fear the reproach of men or be terrified by their insults' " (verse 7, NIV).

Suppose you work in a busy office where there is the inevitable politics. People gossip; unkind words are spoken. Rumors go around and around. And you're trying—sometimes failing, sometimes succeeding, but trying—to act as a Christian. You try to use the tactics a Christian should and avoid the others. Because of that, you endure some insults without being able to retaliate. You feel your face burning, your stomach tightening.

But the Bible promises that you shouldn't worry about an answer to those verbal jabs. If it's needed, an answer will be given to you from a higher power. Matthew 10:19, 20: " 'When they arrest you [for your faith], do not worry about what to say or how to say it. At that time you will be given what to say, for it will not be you speaking, but the Spirit of your Father speaking through you' " (NIV).

Admittedly this is talking about real, physical persecution and arrest. But wouldn't the same principle come right down to that lunchroom, that boardroom, where someone looks at you and levels an accusation? We all think later, after our tongues become untied and our minds work more clearly: "Oh, if I'd only thought to say such-and-such. Oh, if only that particular insult, that rapier-sharp retort, had been in my head! What a ballistic beauty! But now it's too late." Never worry about a missed opportunity to defend yourselves; the Bible says if God wants us to have an answer, He'll put it in our minds at the perfect moment. Most of the time, we should probably thank Him for *not* sending us anything real smart and sassy to say to our accusers. Even Jesus was silent, like a lamb going to the slaughter, until God's enemies challenged Him specifically about His connection to God. Then and only then He spoke Heaven's answer.

How does Isaiah follow up his own advice to not fear being insulted? " 'The moth will eat them up like a garment; the worm will devour them like wool. But my righteousness will last forever, my salvation through all generations' " (Isaiah 51:8, NIV).

In other words, why should *we* yearn to do *God's* job? If any enemy of the faith offends you, especially because of your faith, just quietly remember what his future is and what your future is. God's salvation for you lasts through all generations, and the end result of those who rebel against God is a much more sober matter than anything you and I might be enduring here today.

In that same issue of *Leadership* magazine referred to earlier in the chapter, Pastor Ben Patterson tells about a church in which things were really a mess—politics and frustration and many disgruntled worshipers punching that "three" on the phone. "Your sermons stink and so do you" was the basic mantra going around in the parking lot. And the years ahead in that prison of verbal persecution loomed endlessly before him. "For all I knew, I was going to be serving that church, a job I didn't like, for a long time. That four-year period was about coming to the place where I could say to God, 'To see Your face is so worthwhile that *nothing* in this life is bad enough to outweigh Your presence' " (p. 23).

Isn't that a powerful testimony? Nothing in this world is as *bad* as the presence of Jesus is *good*. Who would punch in a "three" to complain after hearing news like that?

There's a wonderful truth that we find, both in the Word of God and also in personal testimonies. Rabbi Harold Kushner, in his bestseller *When Bad Things Happen to Good People*, discusses how we relate, not just to persecution and insults, but to just plain rotten, bad luck—those incredible strings of bad breaks that hit some people. What does it all mean? Where is God anyway? "I believe in God," he writes.

> But I do not believe the same things about God that I did years ago when I was growing up or when I was a theological student. God does not cause our misfortunes. Some are caused by bad luck, some are caused by bad people, and some are simply an inevitable consequence of our being human and being mortal, living in a world of inflexible natural laws. The painful things that happen to us are not punishments for our misbehavior, nor are they in any way part of some grand design on God's part.

And this is the part that has real meaning for us:

> Because the tragedy is not God's will, we need not feel hurt or betrayed by God when tragedy strikes. We can turn to God for help in overcoming it, precisely because we can tell ourselves that God is as outraged by it as we are.

Notice the powerful truths here. First of all, God is not behind the pain and the persecution. Even the prophets were persecuted; even Jesus received the blows of torment, the spitting in the face. Was that from God? Of course not. There is such a thing as bad luck; there is such a thing as bad people. And yes, just plain and simple we live in an evil world where houses burn down, and sometimes houses of God burn down too—because an evil person with a can of gasoline set it on fire at two in the morning after spray-painting a swastika or an "N-word" on the sign out front.

But, as Rabbi Kushner writes, these tragedies are not God's will! Yes, He permits sin for a time because this is all part of a global experiment, a universally watched demonstration that is fortunately about to end. For reasons that He knows are good and right, God hasn't yet cut short the devil's agenda.

In countries where people are persecuted and killed, God is as angry as we are. In fact, more so, because His own love is far greater than our love. Does God cry at the same funerals we cry at? Yes, He does. When you or a loved one gets the pathologist's report that the tumor is malignant, does He grieve too? Yes, He does.

And your blood gets a bit hot. "Well, why doesn't He prevent the suffering— *if He can?"* We don't know the answer to that question right now. One person is healed and another isn't, and we don't know why. Some Christian preacher lives in Cuba and, like Pastor Noble Alexander, endures twenty-two years in Castro's worst dungeons. Others of us live here in sunny California, glide to church in Ojai each weekend in an air-conditioned Toyota Camry with six speakers of stereo sound, AC, and cruise control. Our life is quite comfortable. Why the imbalance? Why doesn't God set free all the religious prisoners? Why not *right now,* that is? We don't know. But we know that God is angry about the prison bars and the pain and the pancreatic cancer that exist all around us. Our tragedies are His too. He's with us in every moment of sorrow; the insults that hit us in the face strike a blow at Him too.

The bottom line in all suffering is that "the Lord reigneth." No matter what happens, the God of the universe is with you, and the God of the universe is still in charge. King David, who had some moments of real grief—some of them of his own making—writes in Psalm 139: "Where can I go from your Spirit?" Not that he wanted to hide from God's Spirit. "Where can I flee from your presence? If I go up to the heavens, you are there; if I make my bed in the depths, you are there. If I rise on the wings of the dawn, if I settle on the far side of the sea, even there your hand will guide me, your right hand will hold me fast" (verses 7-10, NIV).

In his book *Living Faith,* former President Jimmy Carter writes about persecution and how in 1966, this born-again young man from Georgia decided to run for governor of the state. Surely God would like to have a faithful Christian in the governor's mansion. But not only was he defeated in that contest, he got soundly beat by a man named Lester Maddox, an avowed segregationist. Carter tells how Maddox used as his campaign symbol a pick handle that he personally wielded to keep African Americans away from the restaurant he owned in Atlanta. And this was the man who had beaten Carter for governor!

Jimmy Carter almost lost his faith over that experience. His sister Ruth was a deeply religious person, a minister. And she listened while her brother vented in anger. Then she quoted the second and third verses of James to him. "Consider it pure joy, my brothers, whenever you face trials of many kinds, because you know that the testing of your faith develops perseverance" (NIV).

And Carter responded with bitterness: "Ruth, don't be stupid! I don't want to just be a peanut farmer all my life, but what can I do now? I have nowhere to go. God has rejected me through the people's votes."

His sister replied, "Jimmy, you have to believe that out of this defeat can come a greater life." Carter, not knowing the future, said, "Ruth, you and I both know that this is nonsense. . . . There is no way I can build on such an embarrassing defeat" (p. 202). Ten years later this same man, this persecuted, rejected politician, became America's thirty-nineth president. Good news, he thought! Four years after that, the same voters who put him into the White House pushed him right back out. Now he'd been rejected, not by one state, but by the entire nation!

What did he do? He kept on. He considered it pure joy—well, maybe not pure joy . . . maybe that famous Carter grin did fade just a bit—to face trials of many kinds. But as Jesus Himself instructed us, we're to "rejoice and be glad" when trials come. And President Jimmy Carter went on to help build Habitat for Humanity into a huge, global success. He's written books on diplomatic and spiritual topics, books that have touched many, many lives. He still teaches a Sunday School class at Maranatha Baptist Church in Plains, Georgia. He's determined, in good times and bad alike, to consider it joy to serve the God who always reigns.

How is it for you and me as we join a world in recovering from the blasts of September 11? I invite you to discover, as the psalmist David did, that wherever you are right now, the God who reigns is there with you. Maybe you've gotten a devastating telegram or phone call or email. Someone you love is gone; someone you care about is hurt; someone you need is now sleeping in the Lord, awaiting the future call of the Lifegiver. But God still reigns. He's there with you at the mailbox when bad news arrives. With you at the cemetery when you say a last goodbye.

Ruth Carter was a ministering help, not just to our former president, but to many others. At the end of his book, he writes: "[Ruth's] faith was beautiful in every way. She loved people and devoted her ministry primarily to those who had lost hope in life. No matter what had happened to them, whether it was drug addiction, alcoholism, infidelity, or crime, she was able to convince them to *place the affliction on the shoulders of Christ and in that way to overcome it*" (p. 201).

10

Temporary Triumphs Against Terrorism

Finally, on October 7, the world struck back. "U.S. Launches Attack" was the banner headline in the *Los Angeles Times*. "Missile Strikes Target Key Taliban Sites." In just the first night of conflict, our cruise missiles and laser-guided bombs knocked out most of the available military targets. "There's just not much there to hit," lamented one advisor. "The biggest weapon the Taliban has is a truck."

And almost immediately, the elusive Osama bin Laden appeared on television sets all around the world. The Al Jazeera network showed a lean, glowering man promising that the United States would experience a nightmare that would not fade.

Even before the smoke began to clear from "The Pit" where the two glorious towers had crashed down to ruin, military experts had warned America that there would be no easy victories, no clear triumphs. Every blow will earn a counterblow, every win will be short-lived. The cancer of terrorism will grow back every time.

There was a great story of triumph and faith that took place in my own denomination a number of years ago. Pastor Dick Barron, who served God as a singing evangelist, came down with cancer. And because he was a rather high-profile minister, many, many believers around the country watched and prayed on his behalf. It was a long, agonizing battle, with surgery and radiation and all the rest.

Slowly the cancer that had threatened the life of this godly man disappeared. He got well! Not just into remission—he was cured. And with a collective sigh of relief, the thousands of Christians who had prayed for his healing breathed a second prayer of thanks and got on with life.

It was almost dumbfounding when, just a few years later we learned that this same preacher, Dick Barron, had been killed in a plane crash. And immediately we all had to wonder *Why?* Why would a faithful Christian, who endured months of suffering followed by a miraculous cure, have that restored life snuffed out in one quick moment? It didn't make sense. These many years later, it still doesn't make sense. And we wonder aloud about the workings of God.

Picture that glorious moment when Lazarus comes walking out of his own tomb. One moment ago he was dead; now he's up and around again. Question: Did Jesus Christ simply pull Lazarus barely back across the line? Was he alive—but still needing to go back into ICU or an oxygen tent? Did he walk out of that tomb and straight into a Code Blue, with his cancer or his black plague or whatever illness had struck him down? Of course not. At that moment, with the healing, resurrecting power of Jesus surging through every vein, every artery, every capillary, Lazarus had to be the healthiest man in Bethany. No wonder Jesus turns to the crowd and says: " 'Take off the grave clothes and *let him go'* " (John 11:44, NIV, emphasis supplied). Not "Let him go back into surgery or to the Urgent Care Center." No, "let him go" back to the fullness of abundant life.

However, sooner or later—and this is a sobering thought—Lazarus died again. Mary and Martha and Lazarus, and we have no word to the contrary, all got old. Eventually all three of them, including Lazarus, finally closed their eyes in the sleep of death. Here's a man who, even though Jesus, the Healer, was his best Friend, ended up dying two times.

What do we make of this?

There have been a couple of high-profile medical stories by Dr. Oliver Sacks that made it into the mainstream media; in fact, Hollywood has latched onto them and shared his miracle moments with a wide audience.

In the story entitled *Awakenings,* Dr. Sacks and others began to work with men and women suffering with *encephalitis lethargica,* commonly called "sleeping sickness." These people were basically catatonic; they would sit in wheelchairs all day staring blankly into space. Were their minds working? No one really knew. They couldn't talk, couldn't respond, couldn't even blink, it seemed. Sometimes a hand or arm would jut out at an awkward angle all day, as though somehow the mind had frozen it in that position.

The experiment Sacks tried involved the drug L-Dopa. When treated with this drug, this test group of men and women abruptly woke up. It was almost like a resurrection; at the very least, the story earned the title *Awakenings*. If you've rented this video, you saw a patient, played by Robert DeNiro, who was now awake! Conversing, remembering. The hospital offered field trips, activities, exercises to help them re-emerge into regular life. Before, this patient and others couldn't even feed themselves or care for other physical needs. They were adults in diapers. But now they were able to function, not fully, but certainly at an acceptable level.

Then gradually the L-Dopa, which had worked so miraculously, began to have less impact. Patients started to slip back, just imperceptibly at first, but then more noticeably. Old symptoms began to return. So the medical team increased the dosage. It didn't work. They increased it more. But it soon became tragically clear that the miracle had been short-lived; a whole truckload of L-Dopa wouldn't be enough to stave off the return to the darkness of sleeping sickness. And by the end of the story, the patient played by DeNiro and all the others were back in their wheelchairs, in their diapers, in their state of catatonic blankness.

Yes, this is how things are in a world infected by sin. And it was the same even for Jesus. He resurrected Lazarus, only to have this good friend die again. He healed people of blindness. Mark 10 tells the story of a man named Bartimaeus, who began shouting when he heard that Jesus was going by: " 'Son of David, have mercy on me!' "

And Christ stops right there. " 'What do you want me to do for you?' " " 'Rabbi, I want to see,' " Bartimaeus told Him. Immediately, Jesus restored his sight (verses 47-51, NIV).

At that wonderful moment in time, Christ didn't then hand this restored beggar a pair of glasses. "Uh, here, I'm afraid you'll still need these." Or a box of Bausch & Lomb disposable contact lenses and some saline solution. "I got you up to 20/40 in each eye, Bart, and this will fix you up the rest of the way. Here's a prescription refill slip you can use." No, when

Jesus made a man well, he was perfectly well, completely restored. Bartimaeus had the two best eyes in the entire town of Jericho.

But only at that moment. Did Bartimaeus get old? Did he age? And when he got to be eighty or ninety, did his eyesight perhaps fade again? We don't know, but certainly the day came when those two eyes so lovingly restored by Jesus were closed in death. Even Jesus, while here on this earth, was working in a kind of L-Dopa environment; He could heal, but not permanently. He could restore, but only temporarily. Even His own mother, Mary—if you subscribe to orthodox Protestant theology—eventually got old and was laid to her rest.

So a fair question comes to our minds. Why is healing so limited? If Jesus is the Great Physician, why don't His healings have more permanence than those of this Dr. Oliver Sacks? All the temporary healings on this planet, including those performed by Jesus Himself, make us wonder why even miracles have to come with a disclaimer: "Offer good for a limited time only."

In their book *Letters to God,* compilers Eric Marshall and Stuart Hample include one letter from a young girl named Sarah, who writes: "Dear God, are boys better than girls? I know You are one, but try to be fair." Another young man remonstrates with heaven: "Dear God. I wrote You before. Do You remember? I did what I promised but You didn't send me a horse yet. What about it? Louis."

We smile, but how often have you and I wondered about the times God didn't send our pony either? Even when there are miracles—when young people almost magically have their tumors disappear or when a bleeding disorder suddenly and mysteriously clears up after a prayer session—we continue to live in this sin-stained world. Cancers may leave, and then they may return. And more than one faithful Christian has heard those words from the doctor: "The tests show that it's back."

There are several things we can learn from what seems to be painful reality in these stories. First of all, you and I are living in a world still ruled by sin. And because of sin, there is pain. And sickness. And suffering. And death. And great skyscrapers falling down with thousands of good people trapped inside. Non-Christians get sick; so do Christians. Terrorists die and so do the innocent people they target. As one preacher observed recently, the mortality rate around here is still 100 percent.

And even while Christ was on this earth, He was subject to the *rules* that bind this planet in sin. His own relatives and friends got sick and died.

What we have to keep in mind is that sin and the chief sinner, Lucifer, aren't going to rule this planet forever. Dr. Oliver Sacks couldn't offer people permanent healing, and while quarantined here on earth, neither could Jesus. But the Bible points us to a time when Christ *will* be empowered to fully and completely and permanently provide the healing that is consistent with His nature. Revelation 21:4 says: " 'He will wipe every tear from their eyes. There will be no more death or mourning or crying or pain, for the old order of things has passed away' " (NIV).

And in the next chapter, the final one in the Bible, it says: "On each side of the river stood the tree of life, bearing twelve crops of fruit, yielding its fruit every month. And the leaves of the tree are for the *healing* of the nations" (Revelation 22:2, NIV, emphasis supplied).

In the prophetic book of Isaiah, we read more about healing: "Then will the eyes of the blind be opened and the ears of the deaf unstopped. Then will the lame leap like a deer, and the mute tongue shout for joy" (Isaiah 35:5, 6, NIV).

Now those healings are permanent! Those new eyes will be 20/20 for all eternity. Those crippled legs will empower former wheelchair occupants to run three-and-a-half-minute miles—and keep on running them for the next fifty millennia.

Well, that is wonderful news. But it's our task now to realize that the promise is given for *then,* not for *now.* Permanent healing and eternal life are God's guarantees for *then.*

In a way, that understanding helps us to pray appropriate prayers. Should we pray for healing when we're sick? Yes! By all means. The Bible teaches us to do this. Many Christians, though, have stumbled over this passage found in James 5:

> Is any one of you in trouble? He should pray. Is anyone happy? Let him sing songs of praise. Is any one of you sick? He should call the elders of the church to pray over him and anoint him with oil in the name of the Lord. And the prayer offered in faith will make the sick person well; the Lord will raise him up (verses 13-15, NIV).

And that sounds so clear. If you're sick, bring all the elders and prayer warriors over—and you will, guaranteed, 100 percent of the time, get well. But in this world of sin and sickness, immediate healing is simply not going to happen every time. Many, many good believers, whose faith was abiding and strong, have had to bow down and realize that God is going to answer this prayer *in its fullness* only when Jesus returns and sweeps away the ground rules put in place here by Lucifer. For now, people get sick; people die. Some get well; some don't.

In the meantime, living down here where warranties run out and healings wear out, should Christians even bother to give out Band-aids®? Should we labor for peace when the Bible warns that there will be no peace? Have you ever had the opportunity to do a good deed—but then sagged because of the obvious smallness, the temporaryness of its effect? You could give that panhandler a dollar, but it was clearly going to go for booze. You could mentor a kid in math at the elementary school, but what chance was there, really, that your help would make any difference? And so you passed by on the other side of the road, to borrow a metaphor from the Good Samaritan parable told by Jesus.

Even Christ Himself faced those situations in which people He could help were only out to score temporary benefits. He fed 5,000 people in one great miracle buffet; how many of them paused to really accept salvation? Luke 17 tells about ten lepers who came to Him for healing. The moment they were made well, nine of them just took off running down the road in celebration. Did they pause to connect spiritually with Christ—or even to thank Him? No, they were out of there.

And yet He healed them anyway. And in that generosity, there's a lesson for each of us. In *Awakenings* this patient, Leonard Lowe, is abruptly freed from the "space-time lock" of *encephalitis lethargica* that had kept him frozen in a catatonic state for thirty agonizing years. It's a story described in the classic medical book, *The Man Who Mistook His Wife for a Hat,* by Dr. Sacks.

The scene that steals the show involves a beautiful young girl named Paula. She's the daughter of another patient who has also experienced this miraculous "awakening," so day by day, she's there in the hospital too. And for a brief time in this story, the eyes of Leonard fall on her. He's just come out of the twilight of his frozen years. He's like a child in his emotions, his abilities to walk and talk and think and experience feelings. But in his sweet, innocent way, he endeavors to woo this beautiful girl.

It's plain to the observer on the sidelines that she is miles above anything he could hope for. Leonard is essentially a shy child, standing there on the dance floor, nervously holding his rumpled hat in his hands. But for whatever reason, she graciously permits just a bit of romance to flourish. They dance with each other and go on outings together and trips to the beach. But you get the idea that in her generosity, she's simply "carrying" the relationship. She's being kind; that's all.

And then, toward the end of the story, is the pain-filled falling away. The L-Dopa fails to work. Increased dosages fail to work. The muscle responses start to lock up again. And where Leonard was quite functional before, reasonably steady in controlling his speech and his hands and limbs, now the tremors return with a vengeance.

And then all at once Paula stands there at the door, looking more radiant than ever. And with just a glance, she knows what's happened. After all, her own relative is fading away as well. And she can see that Leonard is on his way back to the prison of full-blown Parkinson's. Another week and he'll be completely catatonic again.

What should she do? Why waste time on a shell of a man who's nearly gone? They could never have a life together, a marriage, a home, children. He's just a few days away from the finish line. She might as well walk away.

But it's unforgettable what actually takes place. She goes over to him, her smile brighter than ever. "Leonard! How are you?"

And he tries to answer, still childlike in his infatuation with this goddess. "I . . . I . . . I'm not so good. I'm not . . . doing so good."

And she quietly brushes it aside. "It's sure good to see you again." She takes his hand; she visits with him. In her kindness, she makes these last moments special, memorable. And then, right at the end, she asks him, "Do you want to dance again? Like we did before?"

And Leonard shakes his head. "No . . . no. I don't . . . I don't think I can." His whole body is shaking painfully now.

But Paula slowly stands up and pulls him to his feet as well. "You can do it." Then she adds: "I *love* dancing with you." And as the music softly plays, and as he shakes, clumsily, the awkwardness impossible to overcome, she holds his hand and gently leads him across the floor. In her strength, she gives him this last moment of manhood, of validity. And she says to him: "This is nice." He nods. "Yeah."

A few days later, he's gone. Not dead, but back in the wheelchair, locked in a frozen stare. A stare that seems to onlookers to be blank, unknowing. But who of us knows if Leonard Lowe might have been remembering—for the rest of his *life*—the tender sweetness of a pretty girl who danced with him and made him feel like a valued, important friend?

And I see this kind of eloquent, perfect tenderness in the life of Jesus. All around Him were people who had suffered their whole lives from a kind of sleeping sickness. In a spiritual sense, everyone He knew down here had *encephalitis lethargica. Nobody* was awake; the whole planet was afflicted, in a catatonic state. In fact, a few times in the New Testament, when He was speaking just to His twelve closest friends, they would shake their heads and say, "Jesus, we don't get it. What are You talking about?" And in those unguarded moments, He would say to them: "Are you still so slow?" Or so dull? And then He would again quietly explain the lesson or the details to His parables. He basically carried them through the whole time of ministry together.

All through this three-and-a-half-year story described in the Gospels, we find a portrait of this loving Savior who was generous in helping people who didn't deserve it. In virtually every case, these moments of outreach qualified under our chapter title "Temporary Triumphs Against Terrorism." Feeding people who wouldn't be converted. Healing the bodies of people who would then withhold from Jesus their souls.

Probably the most exquisite example is that of Judas. Right at the end, when Jesus knows with absolute certainty that Judas has already sold Him out, already made the deal to betray Him, Christ still treats him with royal affection. Jesus says nothing to the other disciples about Judas's treachery; He doesn't belittle him. In fact, there in the upper room, He takes a towel, bends down and performs the act of a servant, washing Judas's feet!

And we ask "Why?" Why bother! Why waste time and energy and love on this traitorous enemy? Judas was a lost man: he knew it and Jesus knew it. Why expend further energy on a moral zero, a lost cause?

Simply because that was the nature, the holy, perfect heart of Jesus. Yes, He came to this earth to save sinners from sin. It was His ultimate purpose to see lost men and women safely into His eternal kingdom. But for the others—the losers, the rejecters (those who rejected Him), the rebels—it was also Jesus' purpose to brighten up and lift their hearts as well. He didn't consider it a waste. If He could give an eternity of joy, He would. If they would accept from Him only a day of it or an hour or just five seconds of a caress, a smile, a kind word, He would do what He could.

We all know the story, the Calvary scene, where Roman soldiers viciously drove the nails into His hands and feet. They picked up that wooden cross and slammed it into the ground. It had to be agony for Christ. But what was His prayer at that very moment? " 'Father, forgive them, for they do not know what they are doing' " (Luke 23:34, NIV).

Did any of those thoughtless, cruel men ever seek God and accept that forgiveness? There's no indication that a single one of them ever turned his eyes toward heaven. They might have continued the rest of their lives in rebellion against this King who was nailed to a tree and hung there just inches away. They might have rejected eternally this generous gift. But Jesus, in His own agony, still reached out to them. As far as He was concerned, He wanted them to be given forgiveness and the promise of eternity and the guarantee of the abundant life created by His own death. They could turn away; most of them probably did. But He would give them all He could: a forever if they chose, and at the very least the Friday-afternoon moment brightened with the realization "This Man cares. He forgives me."

How is it with us, then? Sure, we all want long-term results for our generosity. We don't want to throw our charity dollars down a sinkhole; we don't want our good deeds to be wasted. And so we keep our scorecards. People have to qualify for *our* benevolence.

All well and good, except for the tattered, torn, ripped, shredded scorecards we see fluttering down to the ground at the foot of the cross.

And what the shredded scorecards tell me is this: *We are all pharmacists.* Every child of God on this planet—preachers and stockbrokers and housewives and factory workers—every Christian has been called by God Himself to be a pharmacist.

It's our conviction that the Christian message is one of healing and wellness. A person who accepts Jesus Christ as his or her Savior is going to inherit eternal life and enjoy eternal life. A time will come when sickness and death and all of the curses attached to sin will be gone forever. To the extent that a believer's witness can have a part in participating with God in bringing a fellow human being that experience, we certainly *are* all pharmacists.

But now a reality check. Does every pill and potion give a person eternal life? Quick! Let's all go to the drugstore! But that's not the case, is it? Many times—in fact, here on earth it's all the time—the medicines we receive at the counter when we make our $10 co-payment bring just a temporary respite from symptoms. Flu feelings are driven out of the body, but not permanently. Allergies can be alleviated, but not eliminated. Antibiotics conquer some bacteria, only to succumb later to other ones.

And so when we consider this statement—*We are all pharmacists*—isn't it realistic to accept the fact that often our labors are going to bring only temporary results?

Pastors and Christian counselors have to field difficult questions every single workday. Some are theological, of course. But we also sit across the desk from people who face huge battles with drugs, with divorce, with loneliness. Some have problems with compulsive eating disorders or with memories and scars of child abuse.

And the man or woman of God tries to offer counsel. Certainly an invitation to come to Jesus and seek a living relationship with Him is the core of every reply. "Believe on the Lord Jesus Christ, and thou shalt be saved."

A frightened jailor in Philippi heard that wonderful message the first century A.D., and Acts 16:31 is still the right message 2,000 years later. But people also need immediate help with that drug problem! The lonely person needs to hear that a human friend cares right now. The teenager who's been through five diets and a home breakup and is almost suicidal needs a solution for right now! The single mother who worries about the safety of her only son who is serving in the armed forces needs encouragement at this very moment.

Even when I might provide a purely spiritual suggestion, I know and you know that the people I'm counseling might apply just the tiniest slice of that advice to their lives. Maybe they get a temporary, one-day lift. They try what the Bible says—and things are a little bit better just for a day or two. And then they slip back. Things improve for a week or two as they begin to pray and read God's Word for themselves. And then there's a bit of falling back.

So—*we are all pharmacists!* We have pills to share that bring healing and relief. Permanent healing, if you'll take them. And day-to-day comfort, a momentary lift, if that's all you are ready for today.

Matthew 8 shares a quiet little story of a time when Jesus and His disciples came to visit and rest at Peter's house. This big fisherman must have been so proud to have his beloved Master visit. Only one thing marred the occasion: his mother-in-law was down in bed with a fever. What does the Word of God record? "He [Jesus] touched her hand and the fever left her, and she got up and began to wait on him" (verse 15, NIV).

She felt good enough to get up and fix supper! Jesus took precious time out of His divine mission as Savior to the *world* to cure someone's fever. The next verse says that all sorts of people came to the front door with their illnesses, and He graciously, one by one, made them all well. No mention of a sermon; no making people fill out Bible-study pledge cards before He would give them the temporary gift of healing. No. Jesus, the greatest Pharmacist this world has ever known, had the Bread of eternal life to distribute . . . but He also had some 24-hour nighttime sniffling-sneezing-coughing-achy-stuffy-head-fever-so-you-can-rest-and-have-a-good-morning medicine on Him.

In other words, Jesus, who loved people so much He *ached* to have them eternally in His kingdom, also loved them enough to meet their immediate, even self-centered needs, right down to a migraine headache.

And so, fellow gospel pharmacists, should we. Because when all is said and done, our Lord tells us in Matthew 25 that the very foundation of heaven, the *hallmark* of that Better Land—and the basis on which we will enter there—is how we as pharmacists treat the person sitting next to us on the airplane, on the bus, at the office, or at the dining room table.

Now Christianity is, most of all, concerned with *permanent* cures, with the salvation offer of eternity. If John 3:16 is the church's Magna Carta text, the church certainly isn't in the business of bringing people just a momentary palliative, short-term boost for the coming weekend. "For God so loved the world, that he gave his only begotten Son, that whosoever believeth in him should not perish, but have *everlasting* life" (emphasis supplied).

This was the mission of Jesus Christ. But as we have noticed, Jesus Christ, who longed with a Calvary desperation to bring people eternal life, also spent the bulk of His thirty-two years of ministry just helping blind people see and deaf people hear and lame people walk. He even provided cures for fever. In other words, the love that is the foundation of our faith isn't blinded to the human needs of the moment while keeping its focus on eternity.

Matthew 25 tells the interesting story that all preachers and all operators of church community "programs" and all witnessing travelers on Shuttle-By-United should consider. This is actually the great scene described by Jesus Himself regarding Judgment Day! God, the holy Judge, is measuring the performance of earth's citizens. Will they be saved or lost? Sometimes known as the story of the sheep and the goats, it's told right before Calvary, indicating that Jesus considered it to be a vital, central message.

So the Son of man, who has just come in His glory, sits down on His throne, and the nations are separated into these two groups: the sheep on His right, and the goats on His left. Our big question then: What factor or factors decide who goes where? Verse 34:

> "Then the King will say to those on His right, 'Come, you who are blessed by my Father; take your inheritance, the kingdom prepared for you since the creation of the world. For I was hungry and you gave me something to eat, I was thirsty and you gave me something to drink, I was a stranger and you invited me in, I needed clothes and you clothed me, I was sick and you looked after me, I was in prison and you came to visit me' " (verses 34-36, NIV).

In the wake of the terrorist attacks on America, we could add: "I needed blood, and you donated. I was a firefighter who needed a cup of water and a round of applause as I headed back into the rubble, and you were there to give it. I lost my residence, and you sent in $100 to the Red Cross so that I could have a place to sleep at night."

And these people in the saved column, the sheep, look up in surprise. "Jesus, when did we do that for You? We don't remember anything like that." With great gratitude He tells them, "Whenever you did it for one of the least of My brothers or sisters, you were really doing it for Me" (see verses 37-40).

Is there mention here of witnessing? Of getting people to be baptized? Of giving huge sums of money to the church? No. Just acts of kindness, small moments of *temporary* healing. Glasses of water, meals, clothes, prison visits, funerals attended, prayers said, clinics staffed, shoulders-for-crying-on offered. It becomes clear here that God has put us in this world to bring joy and relief and healing and the quiet comfort of a full stomach to those around us. And Matthew 25 says explicitly that we are going to be judged on that basis!

Is it still important to tell others what a friend we have found in Jesus? Is it a good thing to invite friends to church? Certainly. But the Word of God tells us here that we are called to serve others in an unselfish and unquestioning way, to bring them happiness, whether or not they join the pastor's baptism class the following weekend.

Permanent healing—everlasting 20/20 vision—is the everlasting legacy of heaven. But for right now, a little bit of sight is better than none! The gift of a prison visit is better than none. A meal for the homeless. A cup of cold water. Jesus says these moments, these small friendship acts of what we call "disinterested benevolence"—Christian charity done without over-riding regard for the baptismal pool—are all done for Him. Will many of them lead to the pool after all, to eternal life, to eyesight that lasts forever? Certainly! And that motivates us. But it's not *all* that motivates us.

So be that kind of friend the next time you fly the friendly skies, or drive the busy freeways, or when you walk the halls of your workplace or when you sit at home with your loved ones.

11

"Thank God Life Is Unfair!"

(From a Communion service, shortly after the events of September 11, 2001)

Many times in the past eleven days I have felt, with a stab of pain, the great unfairness of life. On that terrible Tuesday morning, I watched the twin towers of the World Trade Center burning and then collapsing, but in a city 3,000 miles away. There was no smoke in my air. There was unimaginable devastation in New York, but I didn't live in New York. Firefighters were having horrible, wretched days and nights, but I was not a firefighter. Thousands were trapped, or homeless, or dead—but I was still in a comfortable house, with a job and a family and my heart beating and my lungs taking in air. And it felt so unfair.

And then for the next several days, I had to watch on TV as desperate wives and children and husbands and parents held out photos for the camera. "Has anyone seen my dad?" "Has anybody seen my husband? He's such a great guy. He loves our kids so much. He's a terrific father. He plays 'horsie' with all the neighborhood kids. Here's a video clip at our last Christmas party. I'm three months pregnant." And sitting there on the edge of my bed, watching, I would burst into tears over and over. But my family was fine. I was fine. Lisa was fine. Kami and Karli are both California girls.

They're fine. So the way the deck has been stacked, we all have a tremendous amount to be thankful for.

But when we come here to this place, this House of God, on this Communion Sabbath, and we hold in our hands these two small emblems—the wine and the bread—we realize that the playing field is actually level after all. Because these two emblems, given to us by Jesus, remind me that we all have a sin problem. I am a sinner. Lisa is a sinner. Our girls are sinners. You are all sinners. The people out there are sinners. And what that means is that some people died on September 11, 2001, and some people are going to die on other days—but the wages of sin is death for everybody. All of us. Every one of us, in a sense, has a hijacker aboard the plane of our lives. And we are hurtling toward the graveyard. Everybody.

Now, it's true, I would rather live to be ninety-five, like Helen Eckroth here, than to die at forty-six. But in the grand scheme of things, in the light of eternity, forty-six or ninety-five are not great distinctions. Many people died violently a week ago Tuesday, but all death is violence, really. We fight it. We dread it. We weep every time, whether someone has to jump from the 110th floor of the World Trade Center or die calmly in their sleep. It's bad. Death is always the enemy, and the death rate on this planet is still what it always has been: 100 percent. One death per person.

We've all gotten angry these past eleven days because innocent people died. There were three-year-old babies on those planes. Little Zoe Falkenberg. There were good people in those buildings. A priest named Mychal Judge stopped to give someone last rites, and he died himself. And even Jesus, the most pure and innocent Person to ever live on this planet, had religious extremists take Him hostage and kill Him.

So we have this bread and this wine put before us every now and then to remind us that because of sin, life is fragile. We're all marching toward the cemetery on a level playing field.

BUT THEN . . . we take these symbols, and we pick them up, and we express our confidence in the Savior they stand for. And the raw reality is that the playing field is leveled again—and we all can be saved.

In Luke 22, which we always read on these high Sabbaths, Jesus tells us explicitly that this bread and this wine is His body and this blood, and that it is given for us. "This is My body, which is given for you. This is My blood, which is poured out for you" (see verses 19-21).

We do not get eternal life through these symbols, but through Jesus, whom these symbols represent.

It's easy to feel like the New York story is real and that the biblical story comes from Fantasyland. Here on this planet, if it gets on CNN that somebody died for somebody else, then we believe it. I'm sure most of you read about a man named Tom Burnett. He was on United Airlines Flight 93, going from Newark to San Francisco. His plane was being hijacked, and he got his wife, Deena, on the phone in San Ramon, near San Francisco. Jeremy Glick called his wife, Lyzbeth, in the Catskills. Mark Bingham called his mom, Alice, in Saratoga, northern California. Todd Beamer of New Jersey tried to call his wife, couldn't get through, and then called his friends at the office. And we don't know the details—only God knows—but apparently these four men and others decided to rush the hijackers and resist them; and somehow that plane, which was destined for Washington, D.C. and a death rendezvous with thousands, crashed in an empty field in Pennsylvania. They gave their lives to save others.

But I just want to tell you that the sacrifice told about in Matthew, Mark, Luke, and John is just as real as what those men on Flight 93 did. Jesus took some bomb blasts Himself; He allowed every fiery dart from Satan to be taken into Himself. And it's up to us today to think about that, to believe it, to embrace it, and to live it.

I had a phone call that Tuesday morning from a man who comes to this church just once in a while. Every now and then he's here, but he doesn't appear to take it very seriously. And he said to me, "Oh, Pastor Dave, isn't this terrible?" And I said to him, "Yes, it is." And then I reminded him that life is fragile and that this battle is real and that not one of us knows when we will come to the end of our own opportunity to believe in the bread and the wine and to choose Jesus Christ as our Rescuer. So every now and then we want to hold these symbols in our hands—like flags or little miniature United Airlines jets—and cling to the reality that Someone died for us.

Speaking of level playing fields, clear down at the end of the Word of God, Revelation 22:17, Jesus tells us: Everybody. In the highways and the byways. Everybody. "The Spirit and the Bride say, 'Come!' And let him who hears say, 'Come!' Whoever is thirsty, let him come; and whoever wishes, let him take the free gift of the water of life" (NIV).

On the one hand, we have absolute fairness here. The bread and the wine are the great equalizers. These little symbols actually loom taller than the World Trade Center used to do. Without them, we are all lost sinners. Our lives have been hijacked; every one of us. But if we embrace the gift these represent, every single one of us can be saved. We can all lay claim to Calvary.

But of course, when we talk about fairness or unfairness in a cosmic, spiritual sense, there's always the other side of the coin. I've always liked the cartoon strip from Calvin and Hobbes where little Calvin, who is always so picked on, complains to his dad, "How come I have to go to bed so early? *You* don't have to go to bed early. This is so unfair!"

And his dad, reading the newspaper, is just totally cool. "The *world* isn't fair, Calvin." As if that helped anything.

And Calvin goes slinking off to the bathtub, his shoulders dragging in the dust. And he says, "I know. But why isn't it ever *unfair in my favor?*"

And here we are. It's fair that we all have access to the bread and the wine. But it's unfair that any of us should get it. This bread is the most unfair thing I know of. Calvary represents the most stacked deck, the most biased jury, the most unlevel playing field, the greatest travesty of justice the universe has ever seen—and it's all in our favor. Am I right?

Some of you know this marvelous line from an old classic book about Jesus, entitled *The Desire of Ages*. Here it is: "Christ was treated as we deserve, that we might be treated as He deserves. He was condemned for our sins, in which He had no share, that we might be justified by His righteousness, in which we had no share. He suffered the death which was ours, that we might receive the life which was His. 'With His stripes we are healed' " (page 25).

If you enjoyed this book, you'll enjoy these as well:

Rising Above Anger
David B. Smith and *Lonnie Melashenko* team up to provide candid advice and practical help for believers who struggle with feelings of hurt, hatred, and desires for revenge. What do you do when you've tried repeatedly to forgive the person who hurt you, but just can't? Should Christians pretend that what happened to them doesn't matter? These and other poignant questions are addressed in this book written to give Christians the proven biblical principles for dealing with anger, and a picture of God's willingness to take away the crippling burden of our treasured grudges.
0-8163-1855-7. Paperback.
US$10.99, Can$16.99.

Let Not Your Heart Be Troubled
Randy Maxwell. Using the words of Jesus and other Bible writers as a guide, Randy Maxwell leads us on an inspirational journey to assurance in troubled times. Find refuge from worries about terror, death, God's love for you, the end, and more in this little book that encourages us to cling to Jesus in the storms of life.
0-8163-1915-4. Hardcover.
US$9.99, Can$14.99

A God We Can Trust
Loren Seibold. The events of September 11 changed our world forever. What does tragedy teach us about ourselves? About God? Pastor Loren Seibold, a frequent contributor to *Signs of the Times*, grapples with the questions we all have when bad things happen and offers reassurance and hope in a changed world.
0-8163-1928-6. Paperback.
US$11.99, Cdn$18.49

Order from your ABC by calling **1-800-765-6955**, or get online and shop our virtual store at **www.adventistbookcenter.com**.
- Read a chapter from your favorite book
- Order online
- Sign up for email notices on new products

Prices subject to change without notice.